Dakota Boy

Robert Woutat

Dakota Boy

◆

A Childhood in Memory

Robert Woutat

iUniverse, Inc.
New York Lincoln Shanghai

Dakota Boy
A Childhood in Memory

iUniverse, Inc.

For information address:
iUniverse, Inc.
2021 Pine Lake Road, Suite 100
Lincoln, NE 68512
www.iuniverse.com

ISBN: 0-595-28447-7

Printed in the United States of America

For the historical background material in Chapters Two and Three, I consulted They Came To Stay, *a centennial publication about Grand Forks;* Red River Runs North! *by Vera Kelsey, Harper & Brothers, 1951;* North Dakota, A Bicentennial History *by Robert P. Wilkins and Wynona Huchette Wilkins, W.W. Norton & Company Inc., 1977; and* North Dakota, A Guide to the Northern Prairie State *from the Federal Writers Project Series.*

To jog my memory of world events from my childhood years, I relied on volumes 5 and 6 of This Fabulous Century *by the editors of Time-Life Books.*

Sources of quoted materials: Fathers to Sons: Advice Without Consent by *Alan Valentine; U. of Oklahoma, 1963.* Meditations on Quixote *by Jose Ortega y Gasset; U. of Illinois Press, 2000.* W.H. Auden: The Life of a Poet *by Charles Osborne; Harcourt Brace Jovanovich, 1979.* Reason in Society *by George Santayana; Dover Publications, 1990.* Elizabeth Bowen, *from an article in* Vogue, *1955.* Wind in the Willows *by Kenneth Grahame; Barnes & Noble Books, 1995.* The Second Sin *by Thomas Szaz; Anchor/Doubleday, 1973.* "An Older Dude" *by Joseph Epstein, from* Once More Around the Block; *W.W. Norton, 1987.* "Stranger in Paradise" *by Robert Wright and George Forrest; Kismet, 1953.* White Gloves: How We Create Ourselves Through Memory *by John Kotre; W.W. Norton, 1996.* "On Keeping a Notebook" *by Joan Didion, from* Slouching Towards Bethlehem; *Washington Square Press, 1983.* Under a Wing *by Reeve Lindbergh; Simon & Schuster, 1998.*

Thanks

to Marilee Hansen, my wife, who never seemed to grow tired of reading successive drafts, whose suggestions were always on the mark, and whose enthusiasm for this project kept it going,

and to Cliff Caine, Mike Mandel, Sheila Mandel, Deb Gundry, Roy McCready, and Tracy Dethlefs, whose perceptive criticisms made this a better book.

For Philip, Jonno and Tracy

Contents

1

For thousands of years, father and son have
stretched wistful hands across the canyon of time.

Fathers to Sons: Advice Without Consent—
Alan Valentine

I have just this one memory of my father's last year.

He has been released from the hospital after his stroke and he's now in the nursing home where he sits in his wheelchair in the corridor, slumped to one side. A sash across his chest holds him to the back of the chair, keeps him from slumping further and closing off his windpipe. Other old people are propped in wheelchairs nearby.

Since the stroke, he is immobile and mute; his face is frozen, empty of expression. It has also blurred his vision so he isn't aware of my approach, doesn't recognize me until I'm sitting directly in front of him. They've dressed him and shaved him and combed his wisps of thin, gray hair, but he's drooling slightly from the left corner of his mouth.

It's the first time I've seen him since the stroke.

"Hi, Pop. How ya doing?"

My mother is sitting next to him, gently stroking his useless left arm. She's trying to smile but her lower lip is quivering.

"Are they treating you OK?"

I'm prepared for the sight of his all-but-useless body, but I'm not prepared for what happens next. With his good right hand he grips my hand with surprising strength and his eyes bore into mine with unsettling intensity. In all my 46 years we'd never touched except for quick, perfunctory handshakes, certainly never hugged, but now he's prolonging that grasp, not only with his hand but with his eyes. He's staring intently into mine, trying to see beyond my eyes and into my skull, trying futilely to express something his mouth cannot. His eyes are flooded with urgency and frustration, as if he's been saving up thoughts for all these years, waiting for this moment to let them out. But now, crumpled by stroke, he can't do it. He holds my hand and my eyes for a long time, but as expressive as hands and eyes can be, they won't form the words. Defeated, he finally releases my hand

and lets go of my eyes. I don't know what to do. My mother's smile fades and she looks away.

Four months later he was dead.

Today, almost 15 years later, I'm still wondering what he wanted to say.

Silence wasn't exactly new for him. He'd always been reserved, taciturn, private almost to the point of secrecy, at least about his past and his personal life. Oh, yes, I know a little about him from his obituary. And I have a few photos of him at different ages. But I'll never know what he was like as a boy, who his friends were and what kind of games they played. I'll never know whether he ever got in trouble in school, ever did anything illegal or embarrassing or irresponsible or stupid, anything he regretted years later. Was he ever crippled by doubt? Did he ever flunk a test, ever get drunk, ever bang up his father's car? What were his greatest disappointments? Did he have girlfriends, and how old was he at his first kiss?

In the end, maybe this won't be a *real* story at all. Given the quirkiness of memory, given the disjointedness of human life, maybe it will be more a collection of pictures, an album of photos fixed in time, or a series of overlapping transparencies like the ones in an anatomy text, the ones that expose each system of the body in detail, then collectively exhibit the layered complexity of the whole.

"Life must be lived forwards," Kierkegaard said, "but can only be understood backwards." So I become simultaneously a spelunker, lantern in hand, venturing into the cave of memory, and an archaeologist, armed with shovel and pick, preparing to dig around in layers of time, to hunt up remains of a distant childhood, and maybe to find there some understanding of the enigma who was my father.

2

*I am I plus my surroundings, and if I do not
preserve the latter, I do not preserve myself.*

"To the Reader"—

Jose Ortega y Gassett

The past is always meddling in our lives.

Even the prehistoric past nudges us this way or that, can dictate that we live our lives one way and not another. In Eastern North Dakota's Red River Valley, the land of my childhood, the last ice age left a table-flat landscape and a glacial lake the size of Nevada. What's left today, besides a few scattered remnants called Lake Winnipeg, Lake Winnipegosis, Lake Manitoba, and Lake of the Woods, is a 20 to 30 foot layer of clay-like silt transported by the incoming rivers and left at the bottom of that ancient sea. The black, luxuriant earth of the Red River Valley is so rich, they say, that if you plant a nail today it will come up as a crowbar tomorrow. It was largely this soil—the soil and the climate—that chose the kind of people who eventually settled there, that destined them to be farmers, that determined what kinds of crops they'd raise, and what kind of children. So indirectly, I suppose, this is a story about dirt.

And about climate. The quick, blunt truth about my childhood world is that the climate sifts out the soft and the unprepared. The record high temperature is 120 degrees above; the coldest is 40 below. Summer highs of 100 aren't uncommon, and neither are winter lows of minus 20 to 30. Cars have special heaters to keep the crankcase oil from freezing in winter, and some merchants offer electric hookups so customers can plug in their cars and know when they return that their engines will still turn over. Where I grew up, people are so used to low temperatures they don't say "cold" very often; they save it for when the wind chill is 100 below, when exposed flesh freezes in minutes and your head feels like you've eaten ice cream too fast, when cattle freeze to death standing up in the fields, when blizzards shut down highways and towns for days at a time and sheriffs save stranded people by snowmobile.

When I was three, a March blizzard killed 80 people in the Red River Valley. In the mid 60's, soon after I left the state, a passenger train was buried in snow between Fargo and Valley City along the same stretch of track where, 90 years earlier, Custer was snowbound on his way to the Little Bighorn. When there isn't enough snow to cover the plowed fields, the wind whips up a snow-and-dirt mixture called "snirt." Snirt clouds the sky, grinds in the teeth, seeps around weather-stripped windows and doors, and settles into your carpets and furniture.

Sometimes winter skips right into summer, almost bypassing spring; snow melts fast and the rivers swell, spilling over their banks and spreading for miles across the unrelieved flatness of farmers' fields. Twice in my childhood, the Red River spread into our basement, even though the basement floor was 40 vertical feet above the river's edge, and my parents took turns getting up in the night to run the pump in a futile attempt to keep the river outside.

The flood of 1997, the one that was portrayed so dramatically in the national media, was set up by a series of eight blizzards that left a record 98.6 inches of snow that began in mid November of the preceding year, blizzards that were accompanied by average temperatures way below normal. Wind chills of 50 below were common that winter, and there were no midwinter thaws to give relief; from the first of December to the end of January, the temperature rose above freezing only three times.

So when all that snow finally started to melt, the Red River went wild. Eventually the dikes gave way and the normally harmless-looking river down the hill from my boyhood home, a river that's normally no more than 50 yards from bank to bank, began flowing through peoples' homes and ultimately sprawled to a width of 30 miles. As I watched the breaking story from my home on Puget Sound, there on network television was my older brother in tears of frustration and exhaustion; his own dike had broken and the Red River was flowing through his living room, destroying the home he had bought from our parents, the home our parents had built and where my brothers and I had all grown up. Up and down the river, people—my mother, my brother and his family included—grabbed a few belongings and ran, or waded, to their cars. Feeling secure one moment, they were refugees the next. Within a few hours, a town of 50,000 was all but deserted.

Weeks later, when the river subsided and the refugees were allowed to return, many found their homes destroyed. In the lower parts of town, houses had high-water stains just under the eaves. Garages had drifted from their foundations and resettled in neighbors' yards or on top of cars. Hundreds of homes were uninhabitable and later demolished, including the homes in my old neighborhood. Roadsides became piled high with the soggy residue—furniture, major appliances, photograph albums, wood paneling, children's toys, dresses and tuxes for the upcoming prom—and 224 million pounds of debris had to be hauled to the city landfill. One homeowner posted this sign: "Basement apartment, $10 a month, indoor pool, wet bar, Fri. night mud wrestling."

If you need proof of the general unfairness of things, or just little ironies, consider that those people periodically driven from home by too much water also suffer from drought. In the early 1930's, layers of that invaluable topsoil, that legacy of the glacial age, just dried up and blew away in the incessant wind. A local Episcopal priest who had served in Africa said he'd seen more rain in three months in the Sahara than he'd seen in a year and a half in North Dakota. In 1936—not only the coldest year on record but also the hottest and driest—they had only 8.8 inches of rain. Range grasses dried up, forage crops failed, and a third of the farmers lost their property through foreclosure.

For additional discouragement, there have been infestations of grasshoppers. In the late 1800's they came in relentless waves and drove some settlers out of the state. They ate everything green, starting with the crops, and when they'd finished the crops they stripped the leaves off trees, then devoured the twine on sheaves of grain and the wooden handles on farmers' tools. A U.S. Army officer who saw the invasion of 1868 wrote that for more than six hours they passed overhead, flying low, landing everywhere—on the grass, on buildings, on everything—forming gray, crawling masses. They hit people in the face, flew into peoples' eyes, got tangled in hair and clothes. In the small town of Mott in 1933, the grasshoppers were so thick they darkened the sky and the streetlights went on at midday. After they'd laid their billions of eggs, the fields were covered with a living blanket of larvae three to four inches deep, and the sight of the squirming larvae was probably as repulsive as the stench of the dead.

◆   ◆   ◆

The Red River of the North, one of the few rivers of the world that flows northward, originates at Lake Traverse in South Dakota. For its first 23 miles it's called the Bois des Sioux; then, at Wahpeton, North Dakota, it's joined from the east by the Ottertail, and from there on it's called the Red. The Red continues almost straight north, separating North Dakota from Minnesota as it follows the line of the glaciers of so many centuries ago and, taking its time, eventually meanders into Manitoba's Lake Winnipeg, 315 air miles but 750 river miles from the source. The river is rarely more than 50 yards wide, and in spite of numerous bows and curves, it never strays more than five miles from a straight line between source and mouth. From up close—for a boater, say—the river seems anything but straight. But from miles above Earth, it would look like a straight line pointing just a few degrees west of north, with 13 tributaries from the west and 12 from the east. The Red, dropping only 300 feet in the 315 miles from source to mouth, is a sluggish, indolent river; if it were human, it might be arrested for loitering.

The valley of the Red River corresponds to that prehistoric, Nevada-sized lake. But when you're standing anywhere within fifty miles of the river, you certainly don't *feel* as if you're in a valley. You feel instead completely exposed and vulnerable, as if you're standing naked on a table top extending infinitely in all directions with nothing to protect you. Out there on the prairie, as on the ocean, you can see the curvature of the earth. In the distance you might see a neat row of elms or cottonwoods planted by the WPA in the 1930's to keep the valuable topsoil from blowing away, but nothing else limits your view and there's nothing to stop the wind. The Red River Valley, so fancifully termed, is one of the windiest places in the country; only three American cities—Boston, Cheyenne, and Amarillo—have a higher average wind speed. When there's no wind, you're aware of the quiet—to some a blessing, to others an unrelenting curse. And you can't help but be aware of the sky. In parts of the world where it's blocked out by mountains, forests or tall buildings, you may not notice the sky. But in the Red River Valley, there is so much sky that it commands your attention, it dominates your view, and its color, whether blue or gray, becomes the color of your world.

If you aren't used to it, that much openness, that much sky, can be at the least intimidating and at most, oppressive or even terrifying. The army officer who so disliked the grasshoppers in 1868 didn't much like the landscape either. There's "...too much of everything," he wrote. "Too much sky, too much horizon, and definitely too much virgin, bleak prairie land in all directions." An acquaintance of mine from Pittsburgh, one of the soft and the unprepared, felt exposed and vulnerable out there on the prairie; there was too much flatness, too much openness for him. After two years of constant uneasiness, he went back to Pittsburgh where, amid the smokestacks and tall buildings, he felt at peace again. If you're agoraphobic, steer clear of the Red River Valley.

W.H. Auden didn't much like the Midwest either. He referred to it as "an Eliot landscape where the spiritual air is thoroughly small and dry. If I stay here any longer," he said, "I shall either take to mysticism...or buy a library of pornographic books."

One of my high school teachers never tired of telling us how he once stood atop the tallest building in town—the four-story First National Bank building—and spotted a man reading a newspaper in Grafton 47 miles away. I think he meant the story to be evidence of his superior eyesight, but to me it was testimony to the unbroken flatness of the Red River Valley.

◆   ◆   ◆

If you're wondering why people stay there, why they put up with the winter cold and the floods and the landscape and all the rest of it, it's because they've learned to accept severity, to shrug it off in their stoic, taciturn, North Dakota way, as if it were little more than a nuisance. "Keeps the riffraff out," they like to say. And because they're no different from those who continue to live in the paths of hurricanes or forest fires or on faults in the Earth's crust: they stay there because that's where they live, where they work, where they pay their mortgages, where they have friends, where their children go to school. The blizzards, floods, grasshoppers and droughts haven't given them a metaphysical bent; they don't waste time asking *Why*. They don't wring their hands and whine about their condition. "What the hell," they'd say, "life isn't *supposed* to be easy."

And they stay because their days aren't always bleak. On cold, clear winter mornings the snow is so white and the sky so relentlessly blue you count your blessings—as long as your car will start. On still, summer mornings as you linger in bed, you're soothed by the mourning doves cooing and the cardinals whistling from the tops of the elms. And the sunsets: With the vastness of the prairie sky, the sunsets there are grander, more prolonged, more colorful, more dramatic than any you'll see. They're exciting theatrical events, like the thunder storms you can see coming from a hundred miles away—the thunder that explodes and rumbles across the prairie, the rain so thick your windshield wipers can't keep up with it. You might meet a rare tornado there, but there are no typhoons or tidal waves, no mudslides or avalanches, no forest fires or volcanic eruptions. Or crowds. With 90 percent of the state under cultivation, there are only 9.3 people per square mile. If you think hell is other people, heaven is North Dakota.

To outsiders, North Dakota is *terra incognito*, a cold, bleak, isolated void, and in their mental maps of the country the whereabouts of the state is a little uncertain. Most Americans probably couldn't place it on a map. A *Newsweek* article once called it America's Outback. Some locals have wanted to shed that image by shedding the name; a former governor suggested Pembina (from an Ojibway word for high-bush cranberries), Mandan (for the Indian tribe that lived along the Missouri River and befriended Lewis and Clark), or Lincoln. But these ideas never caught on—it would just be a cheap disguise—and as that same former governor said, "Maybe the name serves to keep a lot of weak people from coming here." I suppose it has. But the state has also struggled to dissuade natives from leaving. A state agency once put up billboards along Interstate 90—I saw them as I was leaving, heading west. "There *is* no California. Stay in North Dakota," said one. Another said, "Mountain Removal Project Almost Complete." But the campaign isn't working. In 1997—admittedly, the year of the worst Red River flood—an annual survey by United Van Lines showed that of all the shipments to and from the state, 68 percent were headed somewhere else. North Dakota was leading the country in "out-migration."

When I was at the University there, some members of the men's glee club composed an underground state song to the tune of "Oklahoma."

> *North Dakota, where the snirt lies thicker than the snow,*
> *Where behind each weed you'll find a Swede*
> *And the temp is 43 below.*
> *North Dakota, where each night my honey lamb and I*
> *Sit alone and weep, the meat won't keep,*
> *Because we're running out of lye.*
> *We know we belong to the sod,*
> *'Cause we're good old North Dakota clods;*
> *That's why we sing Eye-yip-eye-odee-ay,*
> *We're only singing, "You're drying up, North Dakota,*
> *By next week you'll blow away."*

Those of us who sang that song so lustily took a sardonic view of the *real* state song, a sentimental number about pledging ourselves to thee with thy prairies wide and free. I suspect the lyricist was probably a long-time resident who, like his neighbors, loved his state in spite of its drawbacks, in spite of the grasshoppers, the floods and the snirt, just as a parent loves his child in spite of its pimples and runny nose, its lapses in manners, its curious hair styles.

◆   ◆   ◆

Are you wondering what kind of people would settle in a place like this, would *choose* to withstand the long, brutal winters, the grasshoppers, the drought, the floods, the monotonous landscape, the unending, overpowering sky? Certainly not the soft or the unprepared.

First were the Indians—the Dacotah, or Sioux, driven from the Minnesota forests by the Ojibway and forced to adopt a nomadic life on the North Dakota prairie where they lived off the buffalo. Next the whites—the French and the Scots, fur traders mainly. The French were led by Pierre Gaultier de Varennes, Sieur de la Verendrye, an early 18th century trapper/explorer hunting for a water route to the Pacific and paying his way with the proceeds from beaver pelts. He got as far south as the junction of the Red and the Red Lake Rivers, which he called *Les Grandes Fourches* and where a few years later he would have been within sight of my father's boyhood home.

Scots like Alexander Mackenzie, Alexander Henry and Lord Selkirk came to compete for furs with the French and built forts and staked out turf along the Red where it's joined north of *Les Grandes Fourches* by the Park, the Pembina, and the Assiniboine.

Many of the French and the Scots mingled with Indians to create a new race called the *metis*, skilled hunters and trappers who had amazing endurance and in winter could cover 50-60 miles a day on dogsled or 30 on snowshoes. Like the Indians, they lived mainly off the buffalo, but they were the first to exploit the rich Red River soil, growing potatoes, wheat, barley, even a little tobacco.

Through the eighteenth and nineteenth centuries the face of the Valley settlers didn't change very much, at least until the fur trade petered out. Until then the rich Red River soil wasn't producing much but prairie grass. Not that the agricultural promise of the Valley had been kept a secret; it was widely known on the East Coast. But there was no quick way to get agricultural products to the far-away markets, so in economic terms the soil was just going to waste, just waiting to be exploited. The picture changed in the late nineteenth century when a new technology was developed for milling wheat and when, in 1872, the railroad finally crossed the Red River at Fargo and linked the once remote region to the mills in Minneapolis and St. Paul. That's when the great land boom started, when the Valley was flooded by immigrants pouring in by the thousands to settle the cheap, fertile land, when the Valley became an agricultural world and took on the character it had in my childhood and still has today.

This wave of immigrants came mostly from northern and eastern Europe, mostly from Scandinavia and Germany, and they didn't fade into the general population as the French and the Scots had earlier. Norwegians, represented fictionally by Per Hansa and his family in O. E. Rolvaag's *Giants in the Earth*, outnumbered all other immigrants in the Valley by far; 120,000 of them came in the decade after the Civil War and another 170,000 in the 1880's. Settling on the rich soil of the Dakota Territory, they withstood their first winters in sod houses heated with nothing but tufts of twisted hay. Herds of cattle smothered in the deep snow and their carcasses didn't appear until spring. Similarly many people like the fictitious Per Hansa simply disappeared in blizzards and weren't found again until snowmelt. Others, without access to medical help or even simple household remedies, died of coughs or other mild ailments gone unchecked. When they died in winter, they were stacked in snowdrifts to await burial until the ground thawed in April or May. Afflicted by loneliness and implacable desolation, some simply went crazy. It was probably not one of those early Norwegian settlers who first uttered the line, "Let the good times roll."

But thanks to the soil and their own durability and stubbornness, most survived and many prospered, and it's their descendents who were my neighbors and who make up most of the population today.

Those first settlers brought with them a bent for farming and the stamina to withstand the climate and the expansiveness of the prairie. They brought the Lutheran religion and such native customs as Leif Erickson Day and *Syttende Mai*, *lutefisk* and *lefse*, *krumkake* and *julekake*. They even published their own newspapers, two in Grand Forks alone. But there were other national groups too, and some of them settled in towns of their own: the Poles in Warsaw and Minto, the Czechs in Pisek and Lankin, and the Icelanders in Mountain, a name chosen either in a fit of irony or a moment of irrepressible longing.

These new immigrants, pushed out of their Old World homes by land shortages, population pressures, or poverty, were farmers, or fishermen who on the prairie had no choice but to became farmers: stoic, taciturn people who were used to working outdoors, who could tolerate the extremes in the climate, who were willing to gamble everything on that deep, rich, black, alluvial soil.

There aren't many signs left today of the earliest white settlers. The French left a few place names: the Bois de Sioux River at the headwaters of the Red, the towns of Belcourt, Bottineau and Rollette, and—just across the Canadian border—the Valley towns of St. Jean Bapatiste, Letellier, and Joliette. The Scots didn't leave many names on the map either; on the Minnesota side of the river there's Caledonia, and on the North Dakota side, McCanna and Edinburg. But the tracks of the Scots have been more durable than those of the French. In 1902, the Old Timer's Association in the little town of Bottineau had 96 Scots on the roster, some having come directly from Scotland, the rest via Canada. When I was growing up in the 1940's and 50's, some Scottish communities were still celebrating Robbie Burns Day, and today the strange Scottish sport of curling is still played up and down the Red River.

But the Scandinavians left the heaviest stamp. In our neighborhood we were surrounded by the descendents of those nineteenth century immigrants from Northern Europe: the Dennisons, the Hultengs, the Hoghaugs, the Thorgrimmsons, the Hansons and the Aldersons.

My high school class of 180 sounds like the Oslo phone book: Gunderson, Halvorson, Ditlovson and Evenson; Bergstrom, Dahl, Branvold and Anderson; Carlson, Erickson, Helgeson, and Kjensrud; Johnson, Johnson, Johnson, and Jondahl; Lindgren, Lagergren, Larson, and Loberg; Lovegren, Lovegren, Olson and Olson; Magnuson, Osmundson, Paulson, and Sorenson; Svedberg, Thompson, Nelson, and Thorfinnson. There were a handful of Germans among us—in our class there were Ganglehoff, Wohlwend, and Schimke, and in our neighborhood the Nehrings and Bonhoffs—and a few eastern Europeans—Weslowski, Stepanek, and Kosmatka; but the Scandinavians were most numerous by far, their names as commonplace as potatoes and wheat. Prudent, guarded, somber and steady, far from effusive or frivolous, through their vast numbers they created the human climate of my childhood world.

As a child, of course, I was as oblivious to the ethnicity of my world as I was to the existence of people to whom blizzards were unknown. Lundgren, Ganglehoff, Weslowski—these were just names to me, as familiar to me as my own. It wasn't until I moved away from it that I learned what was distinctive about my world, that I wondered how those ubiquitous Scandinavians might have shaped my life, that I wondered who I might have become had I grown up instead in the South, say, or among Spaniards, Italians, and Greeks. Or recognized the truth in an observation by Raymond A. Schroth, biographer of another North Dakotan, Eric Severeid: "To grow up in a North Dakota town, it seems, is an experience so radical…that it is more than a clue to the character of anyone who survived."

◆   ◆   ◆

My hometown was not launched with a sense of high moral purpose. The truth is that Grand Forks began with a hangover. In the fall of 1870, when the white population of now-North Dakota was about 500 and the Red River still carried cargo between Winnipeg and Minneapolis, two barges left Minneapolis at about the same time, one of them carrying beer to Winnipeg. The beer barge was in the lead when a storm hit one night and a couple of kegs fell overboard. The second barge, piloted by Captain Alexander Griggs, stopped to pick them up, and by the time he and his crew reached the junction of the Red and the Red Lake Rivers, they were too drunk to go any further and had to tie up for the night. As I said, seasons can change quickly there; that night the river froze over and their barge was iced in for the winter. To survive until spring, they tore apart the barge and used the lumber for shelters. Griggs made a 12 x 12 foot cabin for himself, and at some point he decided that maybe *Les Grandes Fourches* wouldn't be such a bad place to stay. Soon he built a sawmill to produce lumber for more riverboats and barges and for the new houses that started popping up along the riverbanks. In 1871, a telegraph line came to town and a post office was built, with mail arriving twice a week by dog sled or riverboat.

Within a couple of years, the name was Anglicized and Grand Forks was a frontier village with two schools, a flour mill, a Hudson's Bay Company store, two newspapers (One of them, *The Herald*, is still published today; it won a Pulitzer Prize for its coverage of the 1997 flood.) and a blacksmith who with his two-foot tongs, could double as a dentist. By 1878, the population had grown to 450.

Two years later the railroad pushed north from Fargo through Grand Forks to Winnipeg, pretty much securing the town's future. The Territorial legislature boosted the town again when it established ten-day waiting period for divorce, so before long, before Nevada existed, visitors from as far away as Europe flocked to Grand Forks to shed an unwanted spouse. In 1883, the University of North Dakota was founded there, and by the mid 80's Grand Forks even had a white glove crowd, entrepreneurs who had come west with hopes of turning the town into a hotbed of culture and learning. Mimicking their counterparts in the East, they staged formal balls and extravagant weddings, dressed in expensive jewelry and elegant clothes, dined with crystal, linen and china, and rode in elegant carriages. They even built an opera house with an ivory, blue and gold baroque décor, two curving balconies, luxurious draperies, upholstered seats, and specially designed loge chairs. When it opened November 10, 1890, with a performance of *Martha* by The Emma Abbott Opera Company, the place was packed.

But by the late 1930's when I was born, the Valley had been through the Dust Bowl and ten years of Depression, and all the glitter was gone. We were a town of about 20,000 frugal, unostentatious people, the second largest town in the state—close in size, as Plato saw it, to the ideal city state. We had the University with about 2,000 students, a public high school, two junior highs, and six grade schools. There were a couple of traffic lights downtown but still no one-way streets.

Grand Forks—80 miles south of Canada, at the junction of U.S. highways 2 and 81—was surrounded by table-flat fields of potatoes and wheat. Eighty-seven percent of North Dakota was devoted to agriculture, and more than half the state's residents were farmers. We non-farmers—small town grocers and car dealers and physicians and plumbers and teachers and the like—were certainly dependent on the farmers' success. When the crops were good we could all buy clothes at McDonald's Clothiers and cars at Wilcox & Malm; and when they weren't, everyone wrung his hands and lamented for himself and his family and especially for the farmers. For knowing a feeling of community, there may be nothing like growing up in a small town in farm country. And for promoting a need for community, there may be nothing like strife.

The people who raised us—our parents, teachers, ministers, neighbors, mostly descendents of those Lutheran, Scandinavian immigrants—were morally and politically conservative. Earlier, in the fur trapping days when liquor was a form of currency, when you could buy a horse for a nine-gallon keg of rum, drunkenness was common. But starting with statehood in 1889, North Dakota was dry—Grand Forks declared itself dry even before that—and to buy liquor you had to cross the river into wicked, more free-wheeling Minnesota, to East Grand Forks with five times the number of saloons allowed by law.

In 1882, a black man was hanged from the new railroad bridge for allegedly raping a white man's wife, and the Ku Klux Klan had a strong hold through the 1920's, with two of its candidates elected to the school board in 1924. So people who looked too foreign weren't welcomed there. If a black showed up in town he was probably playing ball for the Chiefs, the local Class C team. The only Hispanics we saw were migrant farm workers who arrived each fall to pick potatoes and wisely stayed to themselves in the shacks outside of town. Our parents weren't hospitable to homosexuals either. Or I should say homosexuality. They didn't know any gays, not because there weren't any but because a gay wouldn't dare admit it. There were enough Jews in town for a synagogue but only one, as far as I know, in my high school class. When I grew up it wasn't unusual to hear others tagged as niggers or spics or queers or kikes. (Not to their faces, of course; we were too polite for that. We might disapprove of a group but accept an individual member. "Greenstein is a pretty decent man," we might say, "for a Jew.") And there was a widespread distrust of Easterners too; it was those Eastern Liberals, after all, who were trying to drag us into a war in Europe where we didn't belong and which was no concern of ours.

So that was my world. That's where I was born and where I steered guardedly through childhood, simply accepting the blizzards and the floods and the droughts as a part of everyday life, automatically inhaling the prejudices around me—the distrust of change, the suspicion of the outside world and of people who were "different" somehow—as just another part of the climate. This inheritance—the remoteness, the sometimes-unsparing climate, the agricultural environment, the strictures of mid-century Lutheran conservatism, the posture of defensiveness against the outside world, the post-war prosperity—what part did it play for those of us who grew up there? How did it mark us? And how did it mark one particular boy, the second of three sons born to a young physician and his wife, a boy who very early showed signs of timidity and a cautious approach to his world, who was much less inclined to dive into life than to stand on the shore and watch?

As early as 14 or 15, and even more so in my early 20's, after a college year in Europe, I started to bemoan my origins, to wish I'd grown up somewhere else, that I'd been heir to more worldly beginnings. So eventually I moved away, as did all of my friends, and tried to leave North Dakota behind.

It wasn't until I left the state that I discovered what anomalies we were, we North Dakotans. "Well," people say, "I don't think I've ever met anyone from North Dakota before. The Black Hills, right?" Or, "Oh, yes, I think I drove through there once. It's pretty flat, isn't it?"

With time I realized that trying to shake my past was futile, that in spite of my efforts, like it or not I'd just have to go through life with a certain amount of North Dakota on my shoes. Later, in middle age, I just accepted the time and place of my childhood, even appreciated it, even enjoyed the novelty of being a North Dakotan and found a certain amusement in it. And finally I came to suspect that *all* growing up, no matter where, is a long, futile struggle to overcome one thing or another.

Now, with sexagenarian hindsight, I'm struck by the uncompromising power of distant geological events to mold the dwellers of those plains, to dictate how one earns a living there, to indirectly color the temperament of a whole region, and by the cohesion that develops when its inhabitants are all subjected to the same whimsical forces of nature, whether malignant or benign.

Whoever I am, however many layers of veneer I put on to conceal it, childhood is an unshakable part of me still, and wherever I go, the past—even the ancient past—is just offstage, a ghostly figure still whispering from the wings.

3

Parents lend children their experience and
a vicarious memory; children endow
their parents with a vicarious immortality.

"Reason in Society"—
George Santayana

It's the first day of school and the teacher is reading the role. When she comes to my name, she pauses for an uncomfortably long time, her brow furrowing, her lips trying out different possibilities, and eventually she takes a stab at it:

"*Woe* tat?"

My classmates squeal with amusement.

"*Wow*-tat?"

They squeal again.

"*Woo* tah," I say quietly, embarrassed, repeating the name if necessary, and wishing I had a common, more recognizable name like Thorgrimmson or Bjorn-aby.

It was perennial entertainment for my classmates all through my school years but always uncomfortable for the teacher and me. Later, in the fourth grade, we were to explain the origin of our names. Not knowing but having to say something, I said it was German, and this being just three years after the war, my classmates bombarded me with hisses and boos.

It was years before I knew that our name came from French-speaking Switzerland, and I found it a relief to be able to say I was Swiss, Swiss being a safe thing to be. My father's ancestors came from a village called Sorvilier in the canton of Jura near the border with France.

Not until my early fifties—when my second wife and I attended the annual Woutat family reunion held in the wooded countryside near Sorvilier—did I hear a plausible theory about the origin of our unusual name. I was the first American Woutat ever to attend the event. There were three dozen French-speaking relatives at the picnic that sunny summer afternoon; few spoke English, a few spoke a little German. We grilled pork chops over a wood fire and ate at long, trestle tables, and over numerous glasses of wine I heard this story, told in a mixture of English and French: In long-ago Europe, when a man commonly took as a sur-

15

name the name of his trade—when a carpenter became Carpenter and a smith, Smith—we had an ancestor who earned his living as a builder of arches. The French word for *arch* being *vout,* he became Voutat. (The spelling of the name was changed when it came to America in the mid nineteenth century; in Switzerland it's still spelled with a "V.")

Ever since hearing of Sorvilier, the ancestral home in my mind was a small, charming cluster of white stucco buildings with balconies of heavy, dark wood and windows underlined with boxes of red geraniums, all of it surrounded by high, snowy peaks. Brown Swiss cows wandered the hillsides nearby, and from my imaginary town I could hear the clank of their bells as they grazed on the lush green slopes. The town smelled pleasingly of geraniums and fresh cut hay. But when the family picnic ended and I asked my host to show me my ancestral village a few kilometers away, he hinted that I was ripe for disappointment. "When you see Sorvilier," he said, "you will understand why your ancestors left for America."

The *real* Sorvilier, surrounded not by snowy peaks but by low, tree-covered hills, is a dreary village smelling not of geraniums and the sweetness of hay but of cow manure and a marginal existence. The one- and two-story houses were not so much white as dingy gray; cows stood sadly in small, muddy yards; the streets were empty; the little train station was closed. We drove around town for a few minutes, just long enough to squash my romantic expectations, then headed for the outskirts, driving past an unpromising field of stunted corn and in a few more minutes arriving at the cemetery.

Surrounded by fields of hay, the little cemetery was more carefully tended and more inviting than the town. We walked the gravel paths among the closely-spaced grave sites, almost all of them planted in red geraniums and red impatiens, and studied the inscriptions on the stones. About three-fourths of them bore my strange family name; and there, in the cemetery of Sorvilier where I was surrounded by Voutats, for the first time in my life my name didn't seem like an oddity.

There was another visitor there, a slender, middle aged, gray haired man carrying a green plastic watering can. My host, a Voutat, apparently didn't know him, even though he was a Voutat too. He nodded to a freshly watered grave nearby. "My mother," he said with a sad smile. The date on the stone was recent. He didn't seem interested that I was also a Voutat, that I had come all the way from America—as if we Woutats were legion and returned from the New World on a regular basis. As we parted I wondered softly to my hostess why this man hadn't been at the family picnic, but she didn't know and apparently didn't want to ask, and I didn't press the point. As my father's son, I've gotten used to living with unanswered questions.

The earliest relative we know about is Joseph Voutat, born seven generations ago in Sorvilier in 1672. The next four generations were born in Sorvilier too. But one of these ancestors, the indefatigable Emmanuel Voutat, went to heroic lengths to ensure the survival of our name. After marrying 17-year-old Caroline Marchand on October 23, 1847, he began the habit of producing children, a habit he and Caroline pursued with great vigor for 31 years. In 1874, with the birth of their 14th child, all of them single births, it seemed they were calling it quits; but four years later, when Emmanuel was 55 and Caroline about 49, they ticked off one more.

It was Emmanuel's younger brother Oliver, my great grandfather, who in mid nineteenth century packed his bags and came to America. We don't know why he left; maybe he was intimidated by the role of uncle to 15 nephews and nieces. But my photocopy of his marriage license shows that in 1854 he had arrived in the U.S. and that on August 8 of that year, in New York City, he married a 21 year old Swiss named Jeannette Mettler. At some point he began spelling his name with a "W." He finally settled in Winona, a small Minnesota town on the bluffs overlooking the Mississippi River in a part of the state still known for its scenery as "Little Switzerland." Oliver died in Winona in 1895. At least one other Voutat came to America with Oliver, and today there are little pockets of Woutats in southern Ohio, all spelling their name with a "W," but none has shown interest in detecting a common ancestor. As I've said, we Woutats are an uncommunicative tribe.

My great grandfather Oliver and Jeannette had two daughters and a son. The son, my grandfather, Henry Gustav Woutat, was born in Winona in 1873, studied medicine there, married Aletha Reid in Sauk Center, Minnesota, in 1903, and moved to Grand Forks where he practiced in the Healy, Law, Woutat Clinic.

Grand Forks was a frontier town of 5,000 people then. It had grown quickly since the inauspicious arrival of Alexander Griggs in 1870, and with the coming of the railroad in 1880 its health was pretty much ensured. But then troubles started piling up. A typhoid epidemic hit town in 1885, the result of untreated drinking water, and within eight years there had been about 1,700 cases, 193 of them fatal. At the peak of the epidemic about ten people a week were being treated at the Deaconess Hospital, the same rate at which people were fleeing town. Professors at the University warned repeatedly about problems with the water supply, but nothing was done until 1893 when the city installed a filtering system. That same year the nationwide panic forced the Northern Pacific Railroad into bankruptcy for the second time and strained the town's link with the rest of the world. And soon after that, a Thanksgiving blizzard blew into town and killed six people.

◆   ◆   ◆

I have no photos of my grandfather Henry as a young man, but I do have one taken in his 50's, maybe: He has gray or white hair, neatly trimmed; dark, slightly-arching eyebrows, close-set ears, a small, unsmiling mouth; and the Woutat nose, which is long, slightly convex, and rounded at the end. He's wearing metal-rimmed glasses with round lenses. On his lapel he wears what looks like a Rotary pin.

Henry and Aletha had two children: a son, Philip Henry (my father), born in 1905, and a daughter, Ruth, born four years later. By that time Henry had bought a house at the junction of the Red and Red Lake rivers where the Point Bridge crosses to the Minnesota side, a crossroads in local history. Had my father been there just 30 years earlier, from his backyard he could have seen the flatboat of Captain Griggs and his inebriate crew frozen into the Red River ice. In the summer he would have watched the annual, miles-long processions of Red River ox carts, as many as 1500 at a time, up to 6,000 per year, as they rumbled past his door carrying buffalo hides and furs from the trapping grounds in Manitoba to the markets in Minneapolis. The wheels of these carts, butt ends of logs, turned on ungreased wooden axles (grease would only have attracted dirt and eventually clogged the wheels). With the ear-splitting screech of the wooden wheels on wooden axles, he would have heard these carts long before they came into view, and he would have shut the windows in a futile effort to keep out the noise. In my father's childhood, the frontier past still breathed warmly on the back of the neck.

In 1915, Henry and his partners established the Grand Forks Clinic, an institution that my father later helped expand into the primary medical center between Fargo and Winnipeg.

In 1918, when my father was only 12, Aletha died at age 40. My mother thinks she had cancer, but the year of her death makes me wonder if she wasn't one of the 20 million victims of the worldwide flu epidemic. Henry later married Virginia Trudeau, a nurse at the hospital who throughout their marriage never overcame the habit of referring to him as Dr. Woutat. Henry, my grandfather, continued to practice in Grand Forks until he dropped to the floor with a heart attack while performing surgery and died a few days later at 62. My father never talked to me about him, or about his mother or stepmother—she moved away after Henry died—and he didn't tell much about his sister Ruth, the only member of his family I ever met. If there are pictures of his mother or stepmother, I have never seen them. My Aunt Ruth was always flabbergasted by my ignorance of the Woutat side of my family, but I never understood why; she could hardly have been oblivious to her brother's reticence.

I *do* have photos of my father, thanks probably to the appearance in 1900 of the Kodak Brownie camera, available then for a dollar. In the first picture, taken when he was four or five, he's standing behind the house dressed in a strange-looking garment that makes him look like a young Cossack. The Red River is in the background. His right arm is draped over the bottom strand of a barbed wire fence. He has light hair and a round face with an impish smile, a smile I never saw in other photos or in his adult life. In another, taken at about the same age, he's wearing a large, straw hat and standing on the running board of the family automobile, a Cadillac, one of only half a dozen cars in Grand Forks in 1908.

(On January 1 of that year, his father Dr. H.G. Woutat had sent the following handwritten letter to the Columbus Buggy Company of Minneapolis: "Dear Sir: I wish to cancel my order for a Columbus Stanhope No. 609 which I ordered from your representative last fall. I dislike very much to cancel this order, but as I have made arrangements to buy a gasoline runabout and sell my horse I do not wish to have a new buggy on my hands." For a young doctor just starting his career, H.G. Woutat had reached an enviable level of prosperity.)

My father went to Belmont Elementary School where his mother was a teacher and where the Superintendent himself made regular visits to test the students in reading. At this point in his education he was probably exposed to the McGuffey *Readers*, written in the 1830's and 1840's but still a fixture in schools well into the twentieth century, a five-book series containing lessons in spelling and pronunciation and not-very-subtle stories and verses chosen less for their literary merit than for their usefulness in illustrating moral behavior and the dire consequences of wickedness. Victorianism was animate, hovering darkly over his generation: Discipline in those days was corporal; children were to be seen and not heard; Sunday school teachers promised hellfire for the morally lax.

In the next photo, taken at about age 10, he's standing erectly before the front porch of his house wearing a white shirt, dark knickers, dark knee socks, and high top shoes. He's holding his hands behind his back, his feet close together, and he's smiling broadly, as if freshly praised for some accomplishment.

In those days boys were collecting baseball cards of Ty Cobb, Christy Mathewson, Honus Wagner, and Rogers Hornsby. They were reading the Sunday funnies, which had just begun appearing in American newspapers a few years earlier: Happy Hooligan, The Captain and the Kids, and Buster Brown. And they were reading stories about Fred Fearnot, Nick Carter, and the great Frank Merriwell of Yale, moralistic stories that gloriously portrayed the pure of heart, the doggedly ambitious, the unbelievably brave.

As a boy, my father spent summers at a primitive cabin on a lake in the coniferous forests of Northern Minnesota, 125 miles straight east of Grand Forks. Lake Bemidji, named for an Ojibway chief and made, according to local mythology, by a footprint of legendary logger Paul Bunyan, was an all-day train ride from Grand Forks. Once they'd arrived at the town of Bemidji, they lugged a summer's worth of gear four blocks from the train station to the lake front, then loaded it into a mail boat which ferried them six miles across the lake to the cabin on the remote east shore.

In the early years of this century, the lakeshore was almost completely undeveloped, so when the mail boat dropped them off they were alone for the summer with no running water, no electricity, no indoor plumbing, and no garbage pick-up. They took their water from the lake, and they dug pits in the woods, one to bury their garbage and another to keep their foodstuffs cool. If his lakeside childhood was like mine a generation later, each night in early summer he combed carefully through his hair and checked every part of his body for wood ticks, then pulled off the engorged, maroon-colored insects and held them over a flame til they crackled and popped. He was tormented by horseflies at least through early July and he battled mosquitoes throughout the summer.

My father might have prepared himself for these wilderness summers by reading one of the most popular how-to-do-it books, Daniel Carter Beard's *The American Boys Handy Book*, written in 1882, a book that taught generations of boys how to skin and stuff a bird, how to raise frogs and trap rabbits, how to tie knots for every need, how to make snowshoes and a sailboat, an armed war kite and a Huck Finn raft.

He must have liked these wilderness summers because as an adult he returned to Bemidji again and again, finally building his own cabin on the same shore of the lake less than a quarter mile from where he spent those primitive summers in his childhood.

In his early adolescence, as another photo shows, my father took on an attenuated, slightly gangly look. He's wearing a dark suit with dark knickers, dark knee socks, and high top shoes. He's still wearing his hair combed forward at an angle, letting it fall slightly over his forehead, but now he wears a somber, more adolescent expression. "Don't treat me like a child any more," it says, "I'm almost an adult."

A later picture shows a more mature boy—actually he looks more like a young man—who has finally abandoned his knickers and high top shoes for a Central High School track uniform: spiked shoes, white shorts, and a white, sleeveless shirt known now as a tank top. He's compact and well muscled, like a sprinter—I think he once told me he ran the hurdles—and he's now combing his hair straight back. As if to remind us that the child is father to the man, the high school yearbook describes him as "cool and calculating." Give him a crew cut and he's an earlier version of me.

Some years after he died, my mother told me that during his high school years my father spent summers working on a farm 200 miles west of Grand Forks in rolling hill country near Minot, a farm that belonged to his mother's family. Those were bad years for farmers. When World War I boosted the demand for wheat in Europe, North Dakota farmers borrowed money to buy more land and machinery to plant more wheat; but when the war ended, the demand diminished and wheat exports sank by 66 percent, and from 1919 to 1921 wheat prices dropped by more than half. The demand in this country dropped for *both* wheat and for potatoes, the main crops then in the Red River Valley: A dieting craze, a widespread desire to imitate the rail-thin flappers of F. Scott Fitzgerald's popular novels, was changing American eating habits.

Another drought hit the state about this time; rainfall was below average for much of the 1920's, so in addition to low prices for wheat there was also low production. Banks started failing as early as 1923, and a year later, when my father was at the University of North Dakota, fraternities and sororities cancelled all formal parties rather than seem frivolous in a time of statewide distress. Before the decade was out, 75,000 people, a tenth of the population, had abandoned the state. North Dakota isn't often a trendsetter, but where the Depression was concerned, it got the jump on the rest of the country.

When my father graduated from high school in 1923, you could bypass an undergraduate education and skip directly into medical school. Get an undergraduate degree first, his father advised him, promising to pay for his medical school if he did. So my father enrolled that fall as an undergraduate at the University of North Dakota in Grand Forks, joined Sigma Chi fraternity, and graduated four years later with a Phi Beta Kappa key. He went to medical school at the University of Minnesota in Minneapolis, then returned to Grand Forks to begin his career as a bachelor pediatrician and practice with his father in the Grand Forks Clinic. He stayed in Grand Forks for the rest of his life and continued practicing medicine until he was crippled by the stroke at age 78.

And that's my portrait of his early life. As I look at it from this distance of years, what strikes me most—this is more telling than the portrait itself—is that almost none of the information came directly from him, that it's based mostly on second hand scraps of impersonal information, some from my mother, some from my own research, a lot of it from extrapolation and conjecture. It wasn't until his obituary that I learned he'd been president of the state medical association. He died without ever telling me anything about his personal life—how he felt about his father remarrying after his mother's death when he was only 12, whether he ever regretted becoming a doctor or wished he'd done something different with his life, whether he had unfulfilled dreams, or had known frustration and disappointment.

Why was it so difficult for him to open up and talk with his sons? Was he chronically, pathologically private, or merely self-effacing?

◆   ◆   ◆

On a visit to Grand Forks one summer when I was in my early 50's and my mother in her mid 70's, a white-haired woman beginning to shrink with age, we made the 75 mile drive north to Cavalier to see her girlhood home. My mother had never offered to do it before, nor had I ever asked her to. In my family, we just didn't make excursions into the personal past. So it wasn't until my second wife pushed the idea that I finally began learning about my mother's early life.

She seemed excited about the trip as we drove north on highway 81 past the table-flat fields of potatoes and wheat, through the small, prosperous, Red River Valley farm towns of Ardoch, Minto, Grafton, St. Thomas and Glasston, little clusters of houses and a few stores shaded by elms and seen from the distance first as water towers or grain elevators. As we drew closer to Cavalier I began asking about her childhood. Her reply pretty well choked off any more inquiry for a while. "My," she said, "you're certainly nosy today." I remember thinking she had lived too long with my father.

But once we reached Cavalier, nostalgia seized hold of her and she started to open up. She didn't say much as we cruised slowly along the elm-lined streets, but sights triggered recollections that made her smile, and what she did say was tinged with great fondness. She took us to the park where she played with her friends more than 60 years earlier, and to the family house where her father maintained a beautiful yard and a garden of flowers and vegetables. And she showed us the corner Baptist church where she spent so much of her childhood and, inside, the water tank where she'd been immersed for her confirmation. She viewed these sights with the wide eyes of a child, as if in amazement that they were still there, and seemed delighted that so little had changed in all those years.

Years later I asked her to write down some details of her childhood, and to nudge the idea along I gave her a little paperback book called *How to Write Your Autobiography*. She didn't take to the idea then. "I'm a lazy writer," she said. But a few years later she did; and as I sit in front of my computer today, I hold in my hands six pages of her life, double spaced, carefully typed in script with her manual typewriter on onion skin paper. Most of what I know about my mother's childhood and early adulthood comes from these six pages.

My great grandfather John Alexander McIntosh, the son of a native Scot who immigrated to Canada about 1840, was born near the St. Lawrence River in eastern-most Ontario in 1845. He married Katherine McGillivray in 1868, taught in schools in Pinkerton and Cargill, Ontario, had 12 children in 19 years—including two sets of twins—and at age 45 uprooted his family and emigrated to the Red River Valley in 1893, just four years after North Dakota became a state. They settled in Cavalier, Pembina County, the northeastern-most county in the state, just 15 miles south of the Canadian border.

Cavalier had been established just 18 years earlier by Missouri immigrants who had loaded their belongings in 10 covered wagons and trekked to the banks of the Tongue River just south of the Canadian border. There they built the Tongue River Settlement, later named (and misspelled) Cavalier for Charles Cavileer, one of the first whites to take up residence in the Red River Valley. The main street of the town was originally one of several routes used by hunters and trappers and by the same Red River oxcarts that carried buffalo hides south through Grand Forks to markets in Minneapolis. About the time those early settlers arrived, the population of North Dakota was little more than 2,400. By the time the McIntoshes settled in Cavalier, the state's population had risen to more than 300,000, largely because of the coming of the railroads, the start of the bonanza farming in the Red River Valley, and the great wave of Norwegian immigrants.

The 1900 census record for Cavalier, Pembina County, lists only part of the McIntosh family: Katherine and the six youngest children—Henry, Effie, Paul, Ezekial, Donald, and George William. (A twelfth and last child had died in infancy.) The names are all carefully recorded by hand in the same neat script, all legible except for the recorder's own signature. Few of those early North Dakotans had been born in the state. Most were first or second generation Scots who had migrated to the United States via Canada. All, of course, were white.

Katherine was listed as head of the family. She was 53 years old at the time, married for 31 years. No occupation is recorded so I assume she was a full time mother and homemaker. In the column headed "Naturalization," I find "NA." The census record shows that she could read and write and speak English, and that her home was mortgage-free.

John's and Katherine's five oldest children—John, Rachel, Jessie, Caroline, and John Alexander—were not recorded in Cavalier's 1900 census; they were probably on their own by then. My great grandfather John's name doesn't appear either. My mother thinks he was 140 miles west of Cavalier at the time, in a town called Bottineau where, among many other settlers of Scottish descent, he'd found a job as a teacher, but why his wife and minor children didn't follow him there is a mystery. At any rate, he didn't stay there long; my mother thinks he was fired for his liberal views. He worked next as a teacher and administrator at the high school in Cavalier and later in nearby Neche (population today, 471). While in Neche in 1904, he published a soft covered, 104 page booklet ponderously entitled *Oral or Written Exercises (a self instructor) in English for Busy Pupils in High Schools and in the High School Grades of the Public Schools*. From this little volume we learn a little of what was expected of children in the rural schools of turn-of-the-century North Dakota. "Explain the difference," one exercise says, "between *disobliging* and *unaccommodating, adequate* and *sufficient, duty* and *obligation.*"

J.A. McIntosh, this observer of fine distinctions, died in 1908, but his 104-page booklet survives him, a light, fragile little volume that feels like dust in my hands.

John and Katherine's fifth child, John Alexander—my grandfather—was born in Pinkerton, Ontario in 1873. Alex, as he was known, a short, slightly built Scots/Canadian with a squarish chin, thin lips, and a straight, thin nose, must have followed the rest of the family to the United States. He attended the University of North Dakota, founded in 1884 with 11 students and four faculty members.

By the time he graduated in 1903, he'd made a name for himself as an orator. Given my childhood memory of him as a laconic grandfather in his 70's, it's difficult for me to see him as a young stirrer of the masses; but as a university senior he won both state and inter-state prizes for an address called "The Power and Eminence of Labor", which survives in the form of a brittle, eight page pamphlet published by the Grand Forks *Herald*, a pamphlet now in my hands. *"The germ of power in a man lies sleeping,"* he wrote in that florid, turn-of-the-century style so imitative of the McGuffey Reader and the Frank Merriwell stories, *"nay, lifeless, until he determines to act; then, in the fertile soil of labor, under warm showers and summer sunshine, it grows and develops like a tree, with extending boughs and leafy branches, with fragrant blossoms and at last with generous fruit."* His final paragraph reveals both an ingrained Puritan attitude toward work and a familiarity with *Ecclesiastes*: *"Produce! Produce! Were it but the pitifulest infinitesimal fraction of a Product, produce it in God's name! 'Tis the utmost thou hast in thee; out with it, then. Up, Up! Whatsoever thy hand findeth to do, do it with thy whole might."* After graduating, he moved west to teach in the small Western Montana town of Bonner where, with a population of about 300, there were no masses to stir.

My maternal grandmother, Evelyn Roberts Smith, also a Canadian, was born in Perth, Ontario, in 1882, one of six children of Robert Smith, a farmer and part time figure in local politics. An ancient, peach-colored obituary handed down by my mother tells me that Robert Smith was born on the farm home in Elmsley, Ontario, on the seventeenth of August, 1839. A farmer, he was also the presiding officer of his town for 20 successive years and was elected warden of the County of Lanark in 1889. He died at Riverside, his home in Perth, on April twenty-seventh, 1918, and the funeral was conducted at his home by two ministers, one a Methodist and one a Presbyterian. His wife, Susan Couch, "preceded him to the better land in 1904," as the obituary put it.

Susan Couch Smith, her obituary tells us, *had been a sufferer for years despite the efforts of the best physicians in this country and in the States. She was a woman possessed of a kind and sweet temperament that attracted the young and the old, the strong and the decrepit, to her.* (They don't write obituaries as they used to.) She died September 27, 1904. She and Robert had two sons and four daughters, one of whom, Evelyn, was to become the wife of Alex McIntosh and eventually my grandmother.

Evelyn Smith attended the Collegiate Institute—probably a secondary school in Perth—then trained to be a nurse at Grace Hospital in Toronto. It was while visiting her sister Carolyn Smith Suter in faraway Crystal, North Dakota, that Evelyn met Alex. They journeyed a thousand miles back to Perth to be married on August 10, 1910. Through much of her marriage to Alex she worked as a nurse, either formally or informally, and was destined to become one of those legendary frontier women frequently called on to tend the sick and help deliver babies in the middle of the night. When Cavalier friends and neighbors were ill, "We'd better call Mrs. Mac," they'd say.

By 1912, Alex and Evelyn had moved to Cavalier to start their family. Alex had given up teaching and had bought a general store with his brothers Donald and Ezekial, running the grocery division himself while his brothers managed the clothing, shoes, and dry goods. Over the next eight years Alex and Evelyn had four children and moved from a small house to a larger home. *And that,* my mother wrote, *is where I grew up, where I went to school and became involved in small town life. Cavalier was a wonderful place for growing up; I have mostly happy memories of those years.*

John Alexander McIntosh, my mother's grandfather, died before my mother was born, but she knew her grandmother Katherine. *Grandmother McIntosh was a darling little woman,* she wrote. *She always had gumdrops for us when we visited her. And I will always remember the trip to the cemetery when she died. We were all in horse drawn sleighs and it was bitter cold.* It was late November, 1926. My mother was 11 years old.

All in all, my mother had a total of 15 aunts and uncles—10 on her father's side and five on her mother's. *All my aunts were musical; they had beautiful voices, as did my dad. All of them married except for Aunt Jessie; she remained a spinster. Aunt Jessie taught music, and it was she who gave us music lessons—she taught all of us voice and piano…We all loved music. It seemed someone was always playing the piano.*

Her mother sang in the choir of the nearby Baptist church where she also taught adult Bible classes and played the organ, a job my mother inherited later. My mother attended church services and Sunday school, was a member of the Baptist Young Peoples Union, and went to church picnics and church taffy pulls and to church programs on Thanksgiving and Christmas. I was surprised to read about all those church activities in her childhood because in her adult life I've never seen her exhibit anything resembling a religious sentiment. I think I even detected an aversion to ministers and religion, especially as she got older: When arranging a memorial service for my father, she dreaded the thought that the minister might actually come to her house. So I suspect that whatever her parents' intents, church met more of a social than a spiritual need.

While in elementary school she learned the Highland Fling and danced it for years afterward, especially at festivals and on the back of a flatbed truck in parades, and eventually she outgrew three kilts. *I was good at declamation too,* she wrote, *and I sang in trios and glee clubs and acted in plays.*

I can't remember what year it was that Dad bought a Model T Ford, an open touring car with side curtains that could be attached. What a wonderful invention! In July he'd decorate it for the Independence Day parade. In the fall we'd drive 45 miles to Grafton for Thanksgivings at Aunt Carrie's and Uncle Joe's in mighty cold weather, but we had lots of blankets, and snow was never a problem. We each had our turn at learning to drive the Model T and sneaking off with it while Dad was taking his nap. Sometimes when we went to Aunt Carrie's and Uncle Joe's we took the train, which was always exciting. We sat in those red plush seats with the windows open and the soot and smoke blowing in, and we counted the towns: Hensel, Crystal, Hoople, Nash, then finally—Grafton!

In winter she and her friends wore moccasins to school over heavy wool socks—*we could run like deer over the drifts*—and on Saturdays and in the evenings they went ice skating; *but the big fun in winter was hitching rides on farmers' bobsleds going lickety-split and trying to get off without killing ourselves.* In the summers, Saturdays were festive days in the small towns in farm country—*Dad's store, McIntosh Brothers, stayed open until midnight to accommodate the farmers, and on summer Saturdays the band played and Doris* [her younger sister] *marched with her trombone.*

In the late 1920's, the idyllic small town life my mother remembers with such fondness went up in smoke. The drought and grasshoppers that were ruining farmers throughout North Dakota would also have hurt a small town merchant in farm country. But hardship became more direct, more personal, when the McIntosh Brothers store and the Jennings Hotel, the heart of Cavalier's Main Street, caught fire in the middle of the night and burned to the ground. *I remember seeing the smoke and the flames from our house a few blocks away. As carefree teenagers, we didn't realize at the time what a blow this was for Mother and Dad. And of course the Depression was beginning. Before that, money had never played an important part in our lives. We really hadn't worried whether we had any or not. But things were different after the fire. Dad opened a small grocery store, and Mother got a job with the county as director of the National Youth Administration, which was part of Roosevelt's National Recovery program. I went to work selling tickets at the local theater, and I worked for a while in a farm office program at the courthouse. My brother Bob helped Dad in the grocery store, and Doris got a job at the drug store.*

After graduating from high school in Cavalier in 1932, she spent two years at Mayville State Teachers College about 100 miles south of Cavalier—*somebody scraped up the money for two years*—and took all the business courses she could, waiting on tables in the dining room and working in the library to pay for her room and board.

It was at Mayville that I first encountered Norwegians in large numbers. It was a whole new world for me. Lutherans can't be that different from Baptists, I'd thought; but they sure seemed so to me: They put cream and sugar in their coffee, they ate lefsa *and* lutefisk, *they spread peanut butter on their toast—I'd never heard of that—and they never seemed to lose their Scandinavian accent. I guess those weren't the best two years of my life, but I did learn to dance the polka and the schottische, and I managed to have a good time and make some good friends.*

When she left Mayville in the spring of 1934, she went to work for fifty dollars a month as a secretary in the East Grand Forks law office of F.C. Massee, the father-in-law of her Grafton cousin Evelyn Suter. *I was a pretty dumb legal secretary,* she wrote. *I'd never heard of a summons or a complaint.* After her first year she was given a big raise—ten dollars a month. She lived with her cousin Evelyn and Evelyn's husband Edgar, paying them fifteen dollars a month for room and board, and sent ten dollars each month to her parents in Cavalier.

In the winter of 1935, the gods smiled on me again. A friend of mine got me a date with a young pediatrician at the Grand Forks Clinic—Phil Woutat. We had our first date in February of 1935—we went to States Ballroom and danced! (I can't challenge my mother's account here of course, but knowing my father as I did, the image of him on a dance floor seems unduly fanciful.)

That summer my mother did something strange and puzzling but at the same time admirable and maybe characteristic. At age 21, having never been out of her little world in the Red River Valley, she got on a train alone and headed for the West Coast. She never told me why at age 21,—and at that particular moment in her life, when she seems to have just established herself in a good job and met the man who might well become her husband—she would take what was probably an uncommon step for a young woman in those days and set off across the country by train, alone. I'm guessing that she spent much of that time wrestling with questions about her future—whether she was ready for marriage, and whether Philip H. Woutat, an established physician 10 years older than she, was the right man for her.

This independent, adventurous spirit was something I never saw in her again until more than 60 years later when she'd been a widow for 12 years and had some recent practice at independence, at making decisions on her own not just about homemaking but about investments and buying a car and all those things not expected of wives in her generation. At age 82, when the flood of 1997 forced the evacuation of Grand Forks, whatever long dormant spirit propelled her westward in 1935 was ignited again. As the dike broke and the Red River advanced toward her home, she had just minutes to flee before the roads were under water. Heading for the door, she stopped long enough in the laundry room to grab some clean underpants from the top of the dryer and stuff them into a plastic bag.

With my brother Paul and his family and thousands of others, she joined the caravan of refugees and hit the road, dodging other flooding rivers on their way to dry ground. It would be a month before the refugees were allowed to return so she headed for the West Coast where she just lived out of her plastic bag. She could have bought new clothes, but she didn't. She could have fretted about the condition of her house but she didn't because there was nothing she could do about it. So she had a good time instead. And when the river finally subsided and electricity and safe water were assured again, she went back and negotiated with the insurance adjusters and the carpet installers and the carpenters and put her house back together again.

When she returned from the West Coast in that summer of 1935, my father drove 30 miles to meet her at Crookston, the nearest train station; and that fall—on Friday, November 1, at 9:30 AM—in spite of the many differences between them, they were married in her cousin's living room in East Grand Forks before 25 family members and friends.

The small town newspaper, hungry for every detail, described the scene: *A green mass of Hawthorne banked in front of the fireplace was surmounted with a row of white tapers and a basket of white Killarney roses on the mantle, as a setting for the ceremony. A pink and white color note was added with tall pedestal baskets of pink and white chrysanthemums at either side and with the pink and white pompoms used throughout the rooms.*

The bride's gown was of colonial blue velvet with a short train. The bodice was furnished with a stitched collar marking a high neckline in front and extending to a low V-shaped back which closed with a row of tiny brilliant buttons. Her flowers were a sheaf of white Killarney roses tied with wide satin ribbons.

In the wedding photo both are smiling broadly. It may be the only adult photo in which my father is smiling enough to show his teeth.

After a ten-day honeymoon in Minneapolis, they moved into their temporary home in the Bellevue Apartments in Grand Forks, just four blocks from my father's boyhood home, paying $47.50 a month for three rooms. But it was an inauspicious time, the middle of the Depression. The national per-capita income had fallen to $375 a year, and in North Dakota it was only $145. My father took a cut in pay. A month after the wedding, his father had the heart attack while performing surgery and died a few days later. Banks were foreclosing on mortgages and a third of the state's farmers were losing their property. Even the weather seemed against them; that winter, the winter of 1935-36, was the coldest on record in North Dakota, and the following summer was one of the hottest. The heat was compounded by drought; in 1936 they had less than nine inches of rain. Then came another wave of grasshoppers; in some towns, they piled up four inches deep on the streets and residents built great fires at intersections to control them. With the Depression and the drought, more than 40,000 people fled the state because they couldn't make a living there. War was imminent in Europe.

It might have seemed that Philip Woutat and Helen McIntosh were trying to prove there was no such thing as a bad time to get married and start a family. My brother Paul was born in September, 1937.

In December 1938, the National Tea Company was selling three pounds of coffee for 39 cents and Herbergers was offering girls' "smart new dresses" for $1.00, $1.95, and $2.95. The Grand Forks Rendering Service was advertising in the *Herald* for "all dead and disabled animals (with hides on) such as horses, cattle, calves, hogs and sheep, removed promptly, free of charges. Phone 20." At the Dacotah movie theater, Barbara Stanwyck and Henry Fonda were starring in "The Mad Miss Manton," and at the Forx, John Wayne was playing in "Adventure's End;" the Paramount was showing the Dione quintuplets in their third feature picture, "Five of a Kind."

Wilcox & Malm on North Third Street was advertising this hot item: *Imagine "Tuning In" Weather. It's uncanny—a little dial in this new Nash beauty "tunes in" spring weather all winter long. And with its new terrific 99hp engine, Nash is the best buy in town. Just look at the low price. $923.*

December 8 in Grand Forks was a mild winter day. The temperature at mid morning was 27 degrees above zero, and even though it dropped steadily through the day, it never fell lower than 14.

The next day, the *Herald* printed this little notice: "Dr. and Mrs. P.H. Woutat, a boy, at the Deaconess Hospital." I was named Robert for my mother's brother Bob and Philip for my father.

◆   ◆   ◆

I can't help wondering if their parents advised them against marriage. The mid 1930's promised a bleak future for everyone in the Red River Valley; beginning a marriage then looked inauspicious and reckless. Besides, there were major differences between them—the 10 year age difference, for one, and differences in education and background—his father was a prominent doctor, hers a small town grocer who, although college educated, was ruined when his business went up in smoke. With 20 years of schooling, a Phi Beta Kappa key, and a bent for rationalism, my father was cerebral, "cool and calculating," interested in history, economics, science, and medicine, in matters of the mind; my mother had only two years of teachers college, not to cultivate her mind but just to qualify for a secretarial job. He tended to be withdrawn and reclusive; she was spontaneous, outgoing, fun loving, someone who loved to sing and dance. He liked the rugged life of the Minnesota north woods and had developed an interest in hunting and fishing, which weren't in her background at all. To some, this venture must have seemed doomed from the start. "Get hold of your senses;" they might have warned, "This will never work."

But in proof that opposites attract, they married anyway, and within a year or two they moved out of their three-room apartment and into a bigger home at 1024 Reeves Drive. Within a year or two more, in 1939, before the Depression was over, they built their permanent home at 1205 Lincoln Drive, a large, two story, four bedroom, three bathroom house on the crest of a hill with a commanding view of the Red River 100 yards away. That's where they raised my two brothers and me (my younger brother Don would come on the scene five and a half years after me) and where they lived together happily and harmoniously for almost 50 years.

As I study these contrasting portraits I wonder this: In their brief courtship, was my rational, practical, cool and calculating father swept up in the passions of love, as my mother might easily have been, or did he chart his marital future with deliberation, precision and careful thought? As far as I know, he hadn't an ounce of poetry in him, and he seemed unmoved by music, so it's hard to imagine him dictated to by relentless pangs of emotion. But somehow their lives converged, and somehow, inexplicably, it worked; they lived together for nearly half a century—until my father had his stroke on the operating table while risking surgery for a blocked carotid artery and died in a nursing home a year later at 79.

If a marriage is a converging of streams, we children who result are a blending of waters. In our family's case, and especially in mine, my father was definitely the main channel and my mother the tributary; what flows through me came mostly from him—his cool, detached, rationalistic, calculating approach to the world rather than my mother's spontaneity and irrepressible optimism. I have often wished it were otherwise.

4

The charm, one might say the genius of memory,
is that it is choosy, chancy, and temperamental:
it rejects the edifying cathedral and indelibly photographs
the small boy outside, chewing a hunk of melon in the dust.

Elizabeth Bowen

My mother is pushing me in my stroller. We have walked from our small house on Reeves Drive to keep watch on the construction of our new house at 1205 Lincoln Drive. It's early winter. November. There's no snow yet, but the young trees are bare, and in the cold I'm wearing my powder blue snowsuit with matching cap, the flaps pulled over my ears. My mother is wearing a navy, shin-length coat with a navy hat and matching gloves.

The house is a long way from finished, but the framing is done and the carpenters are working on the roof. Their hammering rings through the chilly air and echoes off the houses nearby. "That will be your room," she says, pointing to the southeast corner of the second floor. "Yours and Paul's." We watch the workmen for a while, but it's too cold standing still for so long, so we turn around and go home.

I proudly carried this memory around for years, ready to display it at any opportunity and bet my life on its authenticity. But a few years ago while looking through an old family album, I found something that undercut my certainty: a black and white photo of a woman—my mother—standing next to a little boy in a stroller. My mother is wearing a dark coat with dark hat and gloves; the boy is wearing a snowsuit as I just described. The trees are bare but there is no snow. In the background is a two-story house under construction.

The boy's head is turned away from the camera. With his head turned, and with his cap and earflaps, you can't get a good look at his face. I slipped the photo from its clear plastic sleeve and turned it over. On the back was a handwritten date: January 1939. Having been born just the month before, it's *impossible* that I could have been the boy in the picture. The boy in the photo *had* to be my brother Paul, born 15 months before me. My memory had tricked me on two counts: What I thought I'd been remembering all those years was not the event itself but a *photograph* of the event; and the experience I was "remembering" was not even my own but my older brother's. I'd seen the photo so many times that over the years it had insinuated itself into my mind and disguised itself as first-hand recollection, a counterfeit recollection I'd been parading around as truth. My imagination had even added color, sound effects, and dialogue. (If you're looking for a metaphor for Memory, the one indispensable source for a memoirist, think of it as an inseparable friend that can't be completely trusted.)

But historical records *will* show this: When I was born in 1938, 68 years after Captain Griggs and his inebriate crew had heedlessly frozen into the Red River and inadvertently started a town, Grand Forks' population had grown to 20,228. It had two railroads, three bus lines, a municipal airport, the North Dakota Mill and Elevator, a university with 2,500 students, a public high school, two movie theaters, an 18-hole municipal golf course and a country club, four traffic lights, and the State Peony Show. There were still no one-way streets. Aside from the State Mill—the equivalent of 12 stories high—the tallest building in town was the four-story First National Bank building, the location of the Grand Forks Clinic. When we were a little older, it was from that dizzying height that we watched one of the town's major cultural events—the University's annual homecoming parade.

Ours was a neighborhood of undistinguished, middle and lower-middle class homes, most of them single story clapboards. Our neighbors were a small business owner, a farmer, a city engineer, a couple of doctors, an orthodontist, a teacher, and the manager of my father's clinic. One block to the west was Lincoln Park with its clay tennis courts and the Lincoln Park golf course, which extended along the river to the south. A block to the north was the "old folks home," a two-story, red brick building where old men in white shirts and ties and straw hats and old women in print dresses sat outside on wooden chairs in the shade of the gigantic elms and watched children speed by on bikes. On that same block was an open field where local residents could rent little patches of ground to raise vegetables—a field which by late summer was thick with corn, tomatoes, squash, rhubarb, and beans, and where I discovered the incomparable taste of vegetables stolen fresh from the garden.

Within these boundaries of my preschool world, the most interesting attraction was right next door—the home of the mysterious, redoubtable, pepper-haired Mrs. Dennison. She lived in a two-story clapboard, cream colored house with an attached garage on one side and, on the other, a stone wall separating the front yard from the back. While I knew the first names of almost all the other adults in the neighborhood, to this day I still don't know Mrs. Dennison's first name, nor do I know if there was a Mr. Dennison. Occasionally a man appeared in her yard to water the grass with a garden hose. He wore a white shirt and tie and a straw hat long after straw hats were in style. But I never learned who he was.

Within that little world, and maybe in the rest of town, my family would probably have been described as "well off." Our house certainly marked us that way, as did my father's profession that, combined with his instinct for seclusion, further set him apart from many others in town. (He actually seemed to *prefer* to keep his distance as a way of maintaining privacy, and I'm sure he would have approved of his memorial service where his family sat by ourselves in a side room off the sanctuary, where we could observe the service without being seen ourselves.)

Our house, although not large by American standards, was a large house for Grand Forks, the biggest in the neighborhood. It was designed in the colonial style, with brick on the first floor front and clapboard above, and in my childhood it was painted white with dark green shutters flanking the front windows. On the ground floor were the dining room and kitchen, a half bath, my father's den with knotty pine walls, and the living room with a fireplace and a picture-window view of the long, grassy lawn rolling down toward the gigantic cottonwoods and the river. Upstairs were four bedrooms off a long, central hall, a private bath off my parents' bedroom, and another bath for my brothers and me. In the basement was a playroom for us children.

At that time, there may have been a few other homes in town grander, bigger, more stately than ours; but I wouldn't have traded for any of them, or for all of them put together; none of them had a river in the backyard.

From our yard, it appeared that Minnesota had thrust a finger of land westward into North Dakota, forcing the river into one of its many bends. For their permanent home, my parents had chosen a riverside lot at the top of a hill right in the middle of one of those bends; from the bank, barely turning our heads, we could look both upriver and down.

Where it slips quietly past my boyhood home on the eastern edge of North Dakota, the Red is a languid river, muddy brown, muddy smelling, a little too wide for a boy to throw a stone across. To adults, it doesn't have much to offer; it's not especially scenic, and its turbidity makes it uninviting for swimmers and water skiers. But to a little boy, the riverside with its waist-high grass and colossal cottonwoods on either bank was irresistibly tempting and wild. When you include the Minnesota side with its tangled brush and the crumbling foundation of a mysterious, long-abandoned home, accessible to us only on ice in the winter months, it seemed to a young boy nothing less than the greatest place in the world. It aroused fear and wonder and it tickled an instinct for adventure; and until my adolescence, when my friends and I were seduced by cars and school sports and girls, it was a wellspring of excitement, a palpable force in my life. I couldn't help but feel a little sad for everyone who didn't have a river in his own backyard.

But to parents it was a perpetual danger, and some of them contrived fanciful schemes to keep their children away from it. The Hultengs across the street told Alf and Dave that creatures called hoolihookoos lived in the river and fed on small boys. Get too close to the water, the parents said, and the hoolihookoos will pull you in. Other parents warned that the river had a sinister undercurrent; it would seize even the most powerful swimmer and drag him down to a muddy death. No one, they said, was beyond its power.

Our father—Pop, we called him—had a less fanciful but equally effective approach. As a practical man raised in the world of science and rational thought, he preferred a kind of laboratory demonstration, so one hot summer afternoon when I was about four and Paul 15 months older (Don wasn't born yet), he apparently decided we were ready for the benefits of empiricism. "Come," I imagine him saying as he started down the long grassy hill toward the river, Paul and I obediently tagging along behind. Even on hot summer days when your shirt sticks to your back, in the shade of the cottonwoods the air is refreshingly cool. It was peacefully quiet along the river; in the heat of the afternoon, the only sound was the ratchety call of a kingfisher. We stood for a while on the bank, not talking, just watching the muddy brown water slip silently by.

Then without saying anything, Pop bent over and picked up two stones, one in each hand, and tossed them underhand into the river a few feet from shore. They hit the water about two feet apart. Each stone made a small *ploonk*, then sank out of sight. They made little dimples on the placid surface, then concentric ripples which quickly washed away in the current. All in a moment, the stones were gone and the surface was smooth again. It was the first of many wordless lessons from Pop: If a stone could be swallowed by the river as surely and quickly as that, I reasoned, then so too could a small boy.

The hoolihookoos, the powerful undercurrent, the vanishing stones—all this evidence pretty convincing to me. I'd never actually *seen* these hoolihookoos with my own eyes, and the placid surface of the river seemed at odds with the alleged undercurrent; but at age four or five, who was I to challenge the wisdom of adults and toy with death? Besides, with my own eyes I'd *seen* the stones disappear, had watched them get sucked out of sight and never come up again. That was enough. So for many years afterwards, in spite of its lure, I had a distant respect for the river.

Pop's demonstration of the river's power came in handy a short time later when Paul and I developed our plan to murder our father. One summer, Pop committed the massive injustice of sending us to bed well before dark, while the robins and cardinals were still singing and we could hear our little friends still playing outside. Mom had gone out for the evening and we figured Pop just wanted to get rid of us. We lay in our beds and steamed. But eventually we got hold of ourselves, and in a calmer, more rational state we reasoned that if justice were to be done, we'd have to do it ourselves. We'd do the only fitting thing we *could* do: We'd murder Pop.

It would be a fairly run-of-the-mill murder, a murder driven by righteous indignation and a passion for justice and revenge. We'd sneak downstairs to the kitchen, find a long, sharp knife, and stab him dead. That was the easy part; the hard part was hiding the body. But that was where the river came in. Since we weren't big enough to lug off the corpse by ourselves, we'd let gravity do the job for us: we'd roll it down the long, grassy hill to the river and just dump it in. The hoolihookoos would take it from there.

Many years later, when Paul and I were adults and had children of our own, Pop admitted that from the other side of our bedroom door he'd overheard us discussing this Oedipal scheme. But if I'd known that he'd eavesdropped on our conversation that night, I'd have been amazed the next day that he was able to go about his business with such nonchalance, that he wasn't more edgy or on guard.

Occasionally we were reminded that the danger of the river was real. A little boy, the only son of friends of my parents who lived several blocks from the river, wandered from home one day and didn't come back. Unlike parents who lived near the river, maybe his parents didn't see the need to invoke figures like hooli-hookoos, or stage demonstration with stones. The police were called, of course, and eventually the search turned to the river behind our house. As I sat by the bank and watched, firemen in aluminum boats cruised up and down the river for days, towing large, ugly hooks through the water. Later divers went down in heavy canvas suits and the spherical helmets with windows in front, but in the muddy water they couldn't see very far.

Finally the bloated little body rose to the surface; searchers found it snagged in some brush along the bank and carefully sifted the remains from the river with a perforated rubber sheet.

Another drowning involved a horse. In the 1940's, teams of men and horses still came to the river in winter to cut blocks of ice for kitchen iceboxes. They'd pull flatbed sleighs onto the river and use long, coarse-toothed saws to cut large blocks of ice that they'd heft to the sleigh and haul away for later use. Once in the heat of summer, I went with Pop to the Grand Forks Ice & Fuel Company, a long, low shed where, to my amazement, and in spite of heat outside, under mounds of damp sawdust were large blocks of Red River ice, 100 pound chunks of last winter still marvelously preserved as if just cut from the river that morning, a tangible illustration of the past overlapping the present.

One winter, one of the horses broke through the ice and drowned. I don't know how they got him out of the water, but he lay dead in the snow for at least a week, and in my little excursions that winter I was pulled by the sight of his large, frozen body lying on its side in the snow, his shaggy brown coat glazed with ice, his open mouth frozen in terror, one large, frozen, unseeing eyeball staring off into space—a lesson on the permanence and ghastliness of death.

During our early years, when the river was still off limits and our parents were concerned for our safety outdoors, Mom—never our father—spent part of her time entertaining us, usually by reading. In our bedtime ritual, we lay in our pajamas beside Mom on our parents' bed, Paul on one side and I on the other, and she read us the stories of Pooh and Piglet and Eeyore, stories which appealed to us because the simple-mindedness of the characters gave us the rare opportunity to feel superior to someone, even it if was just a bear of very little brain. But I never took a liking to Christopher Robin. That androgynous figure in the Shepard illustrations made me uneasy: Boys are boys and girls are girls, and you should be able to tell the difference.

Next Mom introduced us to Kenneth Grahame's *Wind in the Willows*, and following our pajama-ed bedtime ritual, we entered the riparian world of Rat, Mole, Badger and Toad. In one of the passages that engaged my imagination, Mole is taking his first boat ride on the river, with Rat on the oars.

"So—this—is—a—River!" he says.

"The River," corrected Rat.

"And you really live by the river? What a jolly life."

"By it and with it and on it and in it," said Rat. "It's brother and sister to me, and aunts, and company, and food and drink, and (naturally) washing. It's my world, and I don't want any other. What it hasn't got is not worth having, and what it doesn't know is not worth knowing. Lord! The times we've had together. Whether in winter or summer, spring or autumn, it's always got its fun and its excitements."

But as a child I never felt comfortable in Rat's and Toad's world. It had to do with the characters themselves, or with the illustrations. I didn't take to the appearance of Toad and Rat any more than I had to Christopher Robin. And while Pooh and his friends were engagingly soft and furry, the toads of my experience were warty and repulsive, and the illustrations did nothing to make them more attractive.

My problem with Rat was a little more complicated. Unlike Toad, Rat is certainly a likeable character—generous, kind, considerate, a gentleman of the old school. But I'd had some experience with real rats, and there was nothing attractive about them at all. The annual spring floods behind our house dislodged river rats from their homes and drove them up the hill toward drier ground. One year one of these large rodents somehow tumbled into one of our basement window wells and couldn't get out. As soon as we found him, Pop went inside for a gun while I crouched by the well and studied the rat from two feet away—his long, hairless tail, his small, dark eyes, and worst of all, those two long, curved yellow teeth. Pop stood with the rifle butt against his shoulder, the downward-pointed muzzle about three feet from the rat's neck, then fired once. The .22 made a shallow crack. The rat crumpled, then rolled on its side and was motionless. In its death posture, its repulsive features were even more visible, especially the terrible teeth, but now also the long, pink, lifeless tongue. With great seriousness, I reenacted this event numerous times for anyone who hadn't heard the story, first playing the part of my father, standing upright with an imaginary rifle pointed downward, and then the dying rat, lying on my side and twitching faintly in the final throes of death. This was the rat I saw when our mother read *Wind in the Willows*, and that's why I was relieved when we finally came to the end of the book.

These deaths in my early childhood—the drownings of the boy and the horse and the killing of the rat—violent and ghastly as they were, were still somehow less troublesome than two others. When my maternal grandmother died after living with us for 10 years, it was as if she had suddenly and mysteriously disappeared. I never saw my mother cry; there was no family discussion of her death or her life; I was not taken to the funeral. She just vanished. Three years later our first dog, a golden retriever who wasn't even full-grown, died unexpectedly one day in our basement. ("Don't go down to the basement," Mom warned from upstairs when I came home from school.) Again, I was shielded from the reality of death—even from a discussion of death—and strangely, those two invisible deaths became more mysterious and more puzzling than the others.

From Grahame we moved on to Mark Twain, *Tom Sawyer* first, then *Huckleberry Finn*, stories that were far more interesting to me, maybe because they were about people rather than animals. I had more than one nightmare about getting lost in a cave with Injun Joe and about coming into my room in the evening and finding Pap, his own self, waiting to take my money, tan my hide, and lock me up in a deserted cabin by the river's edge while he went off to get drunk and sleep with the hogs.

But mostly we laughed uproariously at Huck's tricks on Jim and at his praying for fish hooks as a test of Godly benevolence; we marveled at his cleverness in posing as a girl to gather intelligence; we laughed at Jim's naiveté about kings and dukes, at the foolishness of the feud between the Shepardsons and the Granger-fords, and at the outlandish schemes to spring Jim loose from the Phelps' farm.

Maybe the book seemed funny because we hadn't yet seen real human cruelty, suffering and deceit. Or maybe Mom left out certain episodes—the murder of Boggs by Colonel Sherburne, Huck's shame after playing the trick on Jim in the fog, the sad and pointless death of young Buck Grangerford. But in our pre-school innocence, *Huck Finn* was as funny as the stories of Winnie the Pooh. It wasn't until I read the book as an English major in college that I saw how pro-foundly sad it is. Later, as a teacher of literature, I read that novel at least 15 times, and each time I regretted that it could never again be as funny as it was when I was five or six.

We always had plenty of books in the house. On the built-in shelves in Pop's knotty pine den, besides his medical books, were books on history, especially the history of North Dakota and the northern plains. And at one end of the living room were built-in, floor-to-ceiling shelves filled with histories, biographies, nov-els, and a set of encyclopedia. In spite of all this exposure, and in spite of my par-ents' habit of reading, as a boy I didn't read on my own, although I liked to *look through* many of those books—especially *Richard Halliburton's Book of Marvels*, a pictorial history of the Civil War with its photos of battlefields strewn with bloodied bodies, and—when I was a little older—*The Family of Man*, especially the photos of young, bare-breasted aboriginal women.

In spite of all this exposure to printed words, by the time I graduated from high school I had read only two books on my own. One was *Black Beauty*; the other was Richard Henry Dana's 1840 travel narrative *Two Years Before the Mast*. At age 10 or eleven, I pulled that book off the shelf and read the whole thing—all 200 and some pages. What I remember about the experience has nothing to do with the story or the writer's style or anything the book might have taught me about nineteenth century sea travel, but my dogged persistence in completing it—a quality that appeared early in my character and never left. It wasn't so much that I found pleasure in *reading* the book as much as I did in having *read* it. But my limited satisfaction was deflated soon afterwards when Pop came home for lunch and heard of my accomplishment. We were sitting at the dining room table with Pop in his customary position at the head.

"Did you *really* read it?"

"Yes."

"The whole thing? Every word?"

The question made me uncomfortable, and so did the silence that followed it. Having just skimmed some of the longer, more boring sentences, I wondered if that meant I hadn't read the whole thing. But I hadn't really skipped any paragraphs, I reasoned, so I decided I *had* read it all, and that it would be unfair to myself to say otherwise.

"Yes. The whole thing."

He seemed to detect some guardedness in my reply. His eyes narrowed a little and his lips tightened into a straight line. I don't remember his praising me for my achievement, and I don't remember his encouraging me to read more; it wouldn't have been like him. In fact I don't remember him saying anything more at all. What I *do* remember is the suspicion on his face, my indelible certainty that he thought I was lying, and the disappointment in not being praised for my accomplishment. Why, I still wonder after all these years, was he—an avid reader of history and a proponent of cultivating the mind—unable to give me the benefit of the doubt, to show enthusiasm, to commend and encourage me at least with words if not a hug? If he wasn't born a skeptic, something in his background had made him one and he couldn't overcome it. He could take nothing on faith; he needed proof. But I was just as stubborn in my unwillingness to give it to him, and so I learned early that I'd either have to get praise from somewhere else or learn to get along without it.

The first bookplate I ever saw showed a nineteenth century sailing ship plowing through a turbulent sea and, at the bottom, a claim from someone named Emily Dickinson that "There is no frigate like a book." Books can transport us to amazing worlds, one of my grade school teachers said. On the basis of my limited reading, I had to agree with her. But as a boy I was too much of a doer for books to have much hold over me, so the imaginary worlds portrayed in print were no match for the real world of my own neighborhood, especially the real world next door, the world of the redoubtable, pepper-haired Mrs. Dennison.

As I saw her in my pre-school years, Mrs. Dennison was a reclusive, unfriendly woman dressed in a perpetual frown. The other adults in the neighborhood were friendly toward children, or at least tolerant of us; but everything about her said, "I don't like little boys. Stay away from my house. Stay out of my yard." But her reclusiveness just heightened the mystery about her and made her property all the more intriguing. Just as everyone should have a river in his own back yard, everyone should have a Mrs. Dennison next door.

What first stirred my interest was the periodic deliveries of coal to her house, a spectator event for me in those preschool years. We used fuel oil at our house, and when the fuel oil truck came, the driver merely unreeled a long hose that he attached to a valve in the foundation. There was really nothing to see. But the arrival of the coal man at Mrs. Dennison's was something worth watching.

The truck backed into her driveway right beside the house, and the man who climbed out was the dirtiest, sootiest, grimiest person I'd ever seen in all my four or five years; coal dust coated his clothes and every inch of exposed skin. He opened the gate on the back of the truck bed, then tilted the bed so the coal rattled loudly to the driveway. Next he opened a square metal door in the cement foundation of Mrs. Dennison's house and, with a long handled shovel, began pitching coal into the opening. The coal made a wonderfully loud noise as it rattled down the metal chute into the darkness of her cellar.

It was a coal man I wanted to be when I grew up. The coal man was the antithesis of Pop. When Pop left for the clinic he wore a hat, a dress suit, and a clean white shirt with a tie, and when he came home in the evening he was as clean as he'd been in the morning. Whatever Pop did when he went to work, I saw nothing to envy in it. I wanted a legitimate reason to be sooty and grimy, and I wanted to be able to make as much noise as he did by unloading the coal and shoveling it down the chute. I wasn't old enough yet to be a coal man myself, but Pop was, and I thought the next best thing was for him to quit being a doctor and to become a coal man instead. That he showed no interest in the idea was another disappointment to me, and if I could have put words to my feelings, I would have said he suffered a deficiency of imagination.

One day when I was a little older I had a justifiable excuse to go to Mrs. Dennison's house, to ring the door bell and actually wait there for her to answer—an act that took unusual courage for me. My mission was to get rich by selling Christmas cards door-to-door, my prospective customers being limited pretty much to the neighbors. The visit produced one surprise after another. The first was that she actually answered the door.

"Yes?" She gave no sign that she recognized the little boy standing in front of her.

It was the first time I'd seen her up close. She had crows feet at the corners of her eyes, and her face was strangely without animation. She wasn't uncivil to me, as I was afraid she'd be; she actually invited me to step inside the small entryway. And that's where I was hit by the terrible smell.

I struggled to concentrate on the lines I'd already rehearsed. "Would you like to subscribe to some magazines? I'm selling magazine subscriptions." I could barely get out my lines; the suffocating, choking stench—I learned much later that it was the smell of ammonia sniffed straight from the bottle—almost made me gag.

"Let me see."

I handed her my list of magazines with the prices attached. My dream was to sell a subscription to *Holiday*—my cut of the annual $12 subscription fee would have been a handsome prize—but I hadn't figured on the reclusive Mrs. Dennison as the traveling type. While she glanced at the list, I put my hand over my nose, pretending a sneeze was coming on.

"Wait here." She went into the kitchen where I heard her rummaging around, and I took a few stealthy steps further into the house for a glance around.

Nothing prepared me for what I saw. While the outside of her house was unremarkable—it was a two story clapboard, a little smaller than ours, well-kept, with a well-maintained front yard—the inside was shocking. Mrs. Dennison's house was alive with cats; there may have been dozens—I couldn't say; there were too many and they were too much in motion to count. Some were prowling the living room, roaming across and behind the couch and chairs and behind the closed drapes. Others were scavenging on the dining room table, licking old food from plates.

Mrs. Dennison suddenly reappeared from the kitchen, putting on a pair of glasses, then studied the list. Her lips moved slightly as she read.

"I don't need any of these," she said, thrusting the list back at me.

I was relieved. If she'd wanted a magazine, I would have had to stay while she filled out the forms. But even though she didn't buy any magazines, she gave me something even more useful: my earliest lessons in social awareness, the discovery that other households weren't at all like ours.

It was less intimidating to explore Mrs. Dennison's backyard, which was more interesting than ours simply because it was Mrs. Dennison's and therefore forbidden. While our backyard was a plain, open, uninterrupted, well-mowed, grassy slope to the river, hers was a series of terraces, banked by walls of large stones, with stone steps from one level to the next and each level thick with tangled, overgrown foliage. On this backside of the house, a stone stairway lead to a padlocked door on the second floor of the garage. To these tangled, jungly terraces and the stairway to the mysterious, locked door, add a menacing, pepper-haired woman who was probably on constant watch for small, trespassing neighbors and who might just as soon snatch them and grind them up and feed them to her cats—or eat them herself—and you have just enough risk to make it worthwhile for a boy to explore.

One summer morning I was prowling routinely through the terraces, crawling on hands and knees under peonies and overgrown shrubs, one ear listening for Mrs. Dennison, the other to the catbirds calling in the lilac hedge between her yard and ours. These investigations were deliciously sensual. There was the cool, damp earth against the palms and the knees, the tickle of cobwebs on the face, the thick, heavy smell of decaying vegetation, and—except for the catbirds and the faint rustlings I made in my stealth—the noise of silence. I was so immersed in it all that while I was crawling around a peony bush, while I was absorbed in the primitive world of the senses, I almost planted the palm of my small hand on a dead cat in the grass in front of me.

It was a large cat, gray and white, and it lay rigid and unnatural. One eyelid was open—the eyeball was lusterless, milky, opaque—and there was a bullet hole in its side. I saw all that in an instant, and at the same time I pulled back in revulsion. In the next instant I abandoned stealth and raced from Mrs. Dennison's yard for home. It was a long time before I went back.

Whose cat was it? If it was one of Mrs. Dennison's, why hadn't she realized it was missing and gone out to search for it? Did she have so many cats she couldn't keep track of them all? Who'd shoot a cat anyway, and why? And why wouldn't anyone have heard the shot? Or was it shot somewhere else and later dumped in her yard? The dead cat only compounded the mystery of the often-glowering, pepper-haired woman next door. I'd already learned that in my family we didn't talk about death, so I never brought it up at home in spite of the many questions it raised. But there was nothing mysterious about death itself, at least not to a child, not when it was right there in front of you, like the dead rat in the window well and the dead horse on the river ice.

Huck Finn would never have pulled back in revulsion at the sight of a dead cat. To Huck, a dead cat would have been a stroke of uncommon good luck, an opportunity. If he couldn't stumble on one as easily as I did, he would have traded for it—a blue ticket, maybe, or an animal bladder he'd gotten at the slaughterhouse—and he'd have used it to cure warts. He would have taken the dead cat and went and got to the graveyard 'long about midnight when somebody that was wicked had been buried. At midnight a devil would come, or maybe two or three. He couldn't see 'em, he could only hear something like the wind; and when they were takin' the dead person away, he'd heave the dead cat after 'em and holler, "Devil follow corpse, cat follow devil, warts follow cat, I'm done with ye!" I wished I could have been more like Huck.

◆   ◆   ◆

Through most of the 1940's, 1205 Lincoln Drive must have looked like a boarding establishment. My mother's parents, unable to make a living in Cavalier since fire destroyed the McIntosh Brothers store in 1928, moved to Grand Forks where my parents supported them for the rest of their lives. Mom's younger sister Doris had moved to Grand Forks with them and was living with us too, so—with Mom, Pop, Paul, Doris and me—we didn't have enough room for both my grandparents. Or at least that was how Mom explained it to me many years later. Alex and Evelyn, at ages 65 and 55, after living together as husband and wife for 28 years, were separated. Evelyn moved in with us and Alex took a room in a private home on South Fourth Street.

This arrangement dated from the time of my birth, so I just grew up with it, thought it normal, and never had reason to question it. Grandma lived with us until her death in 1948, when I was ten. Yet during the years she lived in our house, I have no memory of my grandfather coming for visits, even for holidays, although later, in my teens, after Grandma died, he came every week and was always with us at Thanksgiving and Christmas. Their separation was one of the many things we never talked about in our family. I live with unanswered questions.

When I try to picture my grandmother now, the woman I see has a face more round than oval, with white hair worn close to her head. She wears metal-rimmed glasses. But is it her face I'm recalling from memory, or is it the photo in the small frame my mother kept on her dresser? I remember that she was diabetic, that she injected herself with insulin she kept in a cupboard above the stove, and that she slipped in our basement, broke her hip, and died in the hospital. How can it be that someone who lived ten years in our house is no more to me than that?

Aunt Doris was still in high school when she moved to Grand Forks. She continued to live with us through her high school years, two years at the University, and for several more years while she worked at the First National Bank. Just as everyone should have a Mrs. Dennison next door, everyone should have an Aunt Doris. Doris was a great addition to our household; young, still single, fun loving, with an irreverent approach to the world, she loved bringing out the devil in me. She had an infectious sense of humor that invited others to be her accomplices in mock irreverence and in delight over the mildly naughty. Her humor was particularly engaging to children, and she gave the impression that at family gatherings she would rather hang around with us than with grownups. At a wedding party, she noticed that one of the guests, a five year old boy, hadn't quite gotten the knack of giving the finger—rather than his middle finger, he was using his pointer—so Doris took him aside to demonstrate the proper technique. "If you're going to do it, do it right," she told him. As one of my own sons put it a generation later, "You never felt you had to behave yourself around Doris."

When she left the house in the morning for school or work, I walked with her to the bus stop and kept her company until the bus arrived, chatting amiably as we waited. Then the bus pulled to a stop, the door opened, and Doris climbed the steps and took a seat by the window. When she was safely aboard, I yelled, "Goodbye, you old poop!" Doris would laugh, switch into a fake frown and make a threatening gesture with her fist, then smile broadly and wave as the bus pulled away.

Doris never seemed to tire of telling that story well into my adult life, and I never tired of hearing it, because each retelling helped to maintain the bond I felt with her—a bond she must have felt too, because 45 years later, when she was 67 and had been a widow for many years, she traveled all the way from Florida to Idaho on short notice to attend my second wedding. She was the life of the party, as I knew she would be, and my great fondness for her continued throughout her life, until dementia twisted her into a crotchety, offensive old woman so tragically unlike the aunt I'd known.

Some time during my pre-school years, our phone suddenly stopped ringing at night, and it was at this point, I learned later, that Pop was making a change in his career. It was one of the few stories he'd told me about his personal or professional life. He'd begun practicing medicine as a pediatrician, he said, but one day when in his irritation with a parent he almost swatted a child, he knew he was in the wrong specialty.

He returned to the University of Minnesota 325 miles away to be trained in radiology, and during that period he was gone from home for long stretches of time. In retrospect, his choice of pediatrics was probably one of his few bad choices in life. He was interested in children—his grandchildren, for example—but only in a distant, anthropological kind of way; I'm not sure he really liked them very much. And I can't see him in a therapeutic laying-on of hands. Given his detached, analytical approach to people, radiology suited him better; it allowed him to deal with patients more remotely through the X-ray machine.

Through X-ray technology and the ghostly pictures it produced, he could peer into patients and detect their maladies from a distance; and if radiation were called for, he could call again on the machine as his most essential tool.

Doris and my grandmother weren't the only other members of our household in my earliest years. Off and on we also had maids; once we had two at the same time—Hilda and Myrtl Langruud from Hoople. Maids weren't uncommon then; couples with young children hired small town girls who wanted to try out life in Grand Forks, which for them was a city. At our house they got room, board, and a little pocket money in exchange for helping with the laundry, cleaning, cooking, and looking after Paul and me. This series of maids we had over the years was never an important part of my growing up, but they *were* part of our crowded household in the early 1940's. As a child, I never thought of our house as congested; this was just the way things were. At the time I might have defined "family" as a father and a mother, a couple of kids, a grandmother, an aunt, and a couple of maids. Mom probably liked having a crowd in the house; she likes anything that livens her day. But she suggests that Pop did not. "I don't know how your father put up with us all," she says.

◆   ◆   ◆

In the early 1940's, our parents were listening to Arthur Godfrey on the radio and singing popular songs like "On a Slow Boat to China," "I'll Walk Alone," "Rum and Coca Cola," and "Mairzy Doats." Sixteen-year old girls wearing baggy shirts with the tails hanging out and baggy blue jeans rolled to the knees were wailing hysterically over some 24-year old singer named Frank Sinatra—fainting, tearing at his clothes, begging him to autograph their brassieres. Teenagers' heroes were Louisa May Alcott, Joe DiMaggio, Douglas MacArthur, Clara Barton, Doris Day, Abraham Lincoln, and Florence Nightingale. The number one concern of half the teenage girls in the country, according to a survey by Purdue University, was their figures; 37 percent of teenage boys were mainly concerned with having a good build. A third of young people said that the most important problem facing them was acne. All of which shows that in spite of an event as large and calamitous as World War II, life still goes on at home.

When Germany invaded Poland in the fall of 1939, I was less than one year old; when the Japanese attacked Pearl Harbor, I was one day short of three. Still, I have vivid memories from the later years of the war. Even a four- or five-year old can detect his parents' gravity and sense that something worrisome is going on.

At the end of the work day when Pop came home from the clinic, he and Mom would sit by the big radio in the living room and listen for the news from something called "the front," and there was something in the way they listened that signaled a higher-than-usual level of interest. Names like Omaha Beach and Guadalcanal had no meaning for me, but the expressions on my parents' faces did.

The war became less abstract for me the day I saw the shocking, now-famous *Life* magazine photo of a dead American soldier lying face down on a wet, sandy beach. The photo is in black and white. The water is eddying around his boots and has begun to bury the lower part of his legs in sand. In the pre-television era, it was *Life* magazine more than anything else that gave a graphic portrayal of the war to those of us at home. That photo has stayed with me all my life. For many years I linked it with the Normandy invasion of 1944, when I would have been five years old; I was surprised to discover the photo was actually taken on Banu Beach in New Guinea and published in *Life* in 1942, the year our government ended a ban on photographs of American casualties. If the purpose of lifting the ban was to rally support for the war, it certainly worked with me.

In contrast to the photographs from more recent wars, that World War II photo is pretty tame journalism. The soldier's body is intact. No blood shows. We don't see the soldier's face. If it weren't for the water rising around him we might think he's taking a snooze. But in 1944, that graphic depiction of a dead American soldier was a shocking development in photojournalism, one that made it harder to glamorize the soldier's life and war in general.

In his own practical way, Pop did his patriotic duty. He bought war bonds for Paul, Don and me, helping to raise $49 billion to support our soldiers, and at the urging of the government he took his sole excursion into the world of agriculture when he planted a "Victory Garden" in that rich black dirt down the hill near the river. With one of the more than 20 million such plots in the country, he and other home gardeners produced a third of all the vegetables consumed in this country, even though real, full time American farmers were already producing enough to feed half the world. My role in this venture was to pull barely-formed carrots out of the ground, wipe them off on my pants, and eat them on the spot, dirt and all, thereby saving other carrots for our soldiers at the front.

In those war years, we Americans went on the biggest scavenger hunt in the country's history, collecting anything that could be turned into weapons or somehow used to support the war effort—aluminum pots, old overshoes, rusty baby carriages, even empty toothpaste tubes. In Los Angeles, residents collected 5,000 tons of car tires. By 1942, zealous Boy Scouts had gathered 150,000 tons of wastepaper, which could be used to make packing cartons. Housewives saved bacon grease, which could be used somehow in making ammunition. Nylon stockings, which had just been invented and were all the rage for style-conscious women who couldn't afford silk, were turned into powder bags for naval guns. One old radiator would provide enough scrap for seventeen .30 caliber rifles; one old automobile tire held enough rubber for 12 gas masks; and one old shovel would help to make four hand grenades

In other parts of the country, hundreds of thousands of women were joining men in the factories, helping to quadruple the production of war supplies in just the first year after Pearl Harbor. In some parts of the country, shipyards were furiously turning out entire cargo ships in just 17 days. In other parts of the country, Civilian Defense Corps volunteers were helping protect the nation by maintaining an around-the-clock watch for enemy ships and planes.

But nothing quite like that was happening around us. It's probably not just failing memory—or even a child's obliviousness—but in North Dakota's Red River Valley we were far, far away from much of the heavy preparation for war. There were no factories in our part of the country, so we weren't producing guns or tanks or any other vital equipment needed by "our boys" at the front. Having no factories we weren't going to be bombed by Japanese planes, so we didn't have to hang blackout curtains over our windows at night, and in our land-locked remoteness on the Northern Plains we were far from the danger of German subs.

Still, in spite of the isolationist sentiment of North Dakotans in the prewar years, once we were *in* the war, patriotism was probably as fervid in the Red River Valley as it was anywhere else in the country, partly because we had enemies who were easy to hate, or whom we could be persuaded to hate. The sneaky Japanese bombing of Pearl Harbor violated our sense of fairness. With their sallow skin and slanted eyes, the "Japs" *looked* different from us. They looked *foreign*. And they talked an unintelligible language. On top of that, we had no trail of ancestors to Japan as we had to Europe, so we were more susceptible to our propagandists' portrayals of the Japanese as sub-human beasts. As depicted in the popular press, "Japs" were small, rat-like creatures with buck teeth and slits for eyes. One propaganda poster showed a menacing Japanese face with the text, "Rat Poison Wanted—There's only one way to exterminate the slant-eyes—with gunpowder." Another portrayed a Japanese as a snake with a semi-human, close-cropped head, large, thick glasses, long fangs, and a long, forked tongue. I did my duty and hated the Japanese.

With the Germans it was a little trickier. Some of our townspeople were German immigrants, or descendents of German immigrants. Germans look pretty much like us. Their language was taught in our schools. On the other hand there were those memories of World War I; and those newsreels of menacing, jack-booted Nazis goose-stepping through the streets of Europe, intimidating every-one with their glowering faces and their threatening salutes, and of the maniacal Hitler haranguing throngs of swastika-clad followers who, without much exag-geration, were easily depicted by our cartoonists as cruel, merciless, knuckle-drag-ging thugs. So I hated the Germans too, and my friends and I loved singing along with a Spike Jones recording of "Der Fuhrer's Face," a derogatory song about Hitler and Goebbels, appealing partly because of the numerous Bronx cheers interspersed to denote contempt.

Throughout the war, Red River Valley farmers, necessary to the war effort here at home, went on producing stupendous amounts of grain. Other men and women between the ages of 18 and 36 were ordered to report for military service and went off to fight, and in their front windows at home their parents displayed banners bearing one star for each family member who had gone to war. (Pop was 35 when the war broke out, but as the only radiologist in the upper Red River Valley he was excused from military duty.) With Mom at the piano, the adults sang the popular war songs—"Praise the Lord and Pass the Ammunition," "There'll be Blue Birds over the White Cliffs of Dover," "Don't Sit under the Apple Tree with Anyone Else but Me," and "Coming in on a Wing and a Prayer."

With the enormous quantities of gasoline needed for military purposes, start-ing in 1942 gasoline at home was rationed and the average driver like Pop was entitled to just three gallons a week. Food rationing began at the same time; meat, butter, cheese, sugar—all were in short supply. Coffee was rationed because the U.S. ships that carried it from South America were commandeered for the war effort, and canned goods were rationed because the tin was needed for weap-ons and for containers for the military C rations.

Caught up in the spirit of the time, we children did our part too, periodically filling small Red Cross containers for refugees or individual soldiers. Each con-tainer was smaller than a shoebox and bore the familiar Red Cross emblem. We filled them with items that might somehow help a soldier endure life far from the comforts of home: small tubes of toothpaste and small bars of soap, note pads and pencils, crossword puzzles, needles and thread, and maybe a personal note of thanks from a small child on the Northern Plains who was incapable of under-standing war but somehow sensed that it was a terrible thing, and that some-where far away, brave American soldiers had to stare it in the face.

Finally there was that triumphant moment in the summer of 1945 when we learned of the surrender of Japan and the end of a war that had gone on longer than I could remember. In other parts of our country—Times Square in New York, for example—people celebrated by getting drunk and kissing complete strangers in the street. In Grand Forks we celebrated by coming out of our homes and honking our car horns. Looking back, it seems like a timid gesture, comically inadequate to the greatness of the moment, but that's what we did. On an ordinary day, I didn't have permission to climb into the family car—a green Dodge with wooden bumpers (domestic steel was scarce during the war)—lean on the horn, and make as much noise as I could. But on that sunny afternoon of August 14, 1945, I did.

The war was only a vicarious experience for us, of course, but it was a deeply moving one. Probably more than any national event since then, for four years World War II pulled us together in a common cause and on a great mission against a terrible menace and ignited us with a feeling of shared purpose. Nothing in this country since then has had that effect. There were moments in the heyday of space exploration—our landing on the moon was one—when we knew a common feeling of wonder and pride. And there were the Kennedy and King assassinations to draw us together in helplessness, disappointment and sorrow. But World War II brought us together on a much grander scale. For four years it energized us politically, economically, nationally and spiritually. The effect was so great that even a small boy in the remoteness of North Dakota's Red River Valley fervently believed that he was playing a part in the outcome of a world struggle, that by peeling tinfoil from gum wrappers, by flattening tin cans and old tubes of toothpaste, he was doing his part to bring down Hirohito, Mussolini, and Hitler. It was heady stuff.

◆   ◆   ◆

Poking further into the cave of memory, I find a few other scattered fragments from those distant years, scraps of my childhood that have refused to go away, one of which is my early surgeries. I was going to have a tonsillectomy, my parents explained, and they prepared me for the event: "Tonsils are useless little things in the throat that can cause illnesses later in life; it makes sense to go to the hospital and have a doctor take them out when you're young," they said. "You won't feel a thing. You'll be asleep." On that understanding I went to Deaconess Hospital with no particular fear, only a slight uneasiness mixed with curiosity and a readiness to have it over with.

I was placed on a bed or padded table with bright lights above me, solicitous figures in white busied themselves around me, a rubber cone was placed over my nose and mouth, and I began counting to 10.

Later, in the slow, blurry process of regaining consciousness, I became aware of the soreness in my throat, a soreness that made it difficult to talk and to swallow the strawberry ice cream they'd given me as a reward. It was later still when I discovered I had lost something more than my tonsils. My little penis was enclosed in a sheath of bloody gauze. With tip of thumb and index finger I cautiously peeled it back and experienced—what? Pain? I remember no pain in the aftermath of this operation. Alarm? Certainly. Puzzlement? Definitely. Surprise? Emphatically. This hadn't been part of the deal. In retrospect, I probably would have preferred my circumcision be done—if it *had* to be done at all—in my infancy, when I'd have been oblivious to it all. But whatever my age at that point—I was probably about five—I wasn't old enough to have developed any symbolic attachment to my penis or to sense any loss in its alteration. As far as I could tell, it still seemed to serve the sole purpose for which it had been designed.

◆   ◆   ◆

In September of 1944, almost all my neighborhood friends trudged off to school and left me behind. I wouldn't be six until December and couldn't start school until the following year. That nine-month period until the following June was the longest, loneliest, emptiest, most miserable part of my childhood. Not very resourceful or inventive as a boy, and a long way from discovering the pleasure of solitude, I was a relentless burden on Mom that year, burdensomely hanging around and asking a thousand times a day, "What is there to *do*?" But Mom had more pressing business at the time, having just given birth in June to my younger brother Don. Unlike Pop, she was never impatient or angry with me, then or ever. "Why don't you go out and play?" she always said calmly.

In my loneliness of that last preschool year, I even began looking forward to the mid morning arrival of the milkman. Anachronistically, Minnesota Dairy still delivered milk by horse-drawn wagon, but at that age it wasn't so much the horse and wagon that caught my interest but what the horse did after he arrived. The milkman would pull the horse to a stop in front of our house and take the fresh milk to the side door, the glass bottles rattling in his metal carrier. Meanwhile I was keeping my eyes on the horse, more specifically on the horse's gargantuan penis—another penis story already?—because it almost never failed that the horse's arrival at our house coincided with his need to empty his bladder. When the yellow stream started, it was thick and prolonged, splattering loudly on the pavement, then flowing heavily toward the metal grate at the curb just a couple of feet from me. I contrasted his equipment with mine, marveling not just at the size but at the time he took to empty himself, and felt what was probably my first experience with awe. But when the driver flicked the reins and moved on, the show was over and I had to look for something else to do.

On Sunday afternoons, a replica of a nineteenth century sternwheeler churned past our house carrying people on short excursions up the river and back. I could sit in the backyard and wave to the passengers as they waved at me. But like the visit from the milk wagon, that didn't last very long, and soon I was looking for something to do again. The longing for human companionship and warmth is a throbbing emptiness, and often the ones who suffer it most are the ones least able to overcome it on their own.

That year, I spent part of each weekday in kindergarten, an experience that not only failed to fill the emptiness but actually compounded my unhappiness. The nearest kindergarten was in the basement of Belmont Elementary School, the same school Pop had attended as a child, and to get there I had to take the city bus alone. Mom accompanied me on my inaugural trip up Belmont Road, sitting next to me in the front seat where I had a good view of the cross streets coming up and where she could point out landmarks I'd need.

"There's a street sign on each corner. Do you see the green sign? That one says Tenth Street. The next one will be Ninth."

I looked for these signs with great apprehension, knowing that next time I'd have to do this on my own. Would I remember how? Would I recognize the signs in time?

"The numbers are getting smaller. Just count backwards. See? There's Sixth. Next will be Fifth and then Fourth, and that's where you'll get off."

I was never able to make the journey alone without fear. Later, as a college student, I traveled throughout Europe on my own. As an adult, I've trekked thousands of mountain miles through grizzly country; I've led groups of adolescents through remote wilderness areas in temperatures of 30 below zero; I've explored several other continents and numerous other countries whose languages I didn't speak. But none of those travels unnerved me like those solitary bus rides in my own hometown at the age of six. Fearing I wouldn't recognize my stop when I came to it, that I wouldn't ring the buzzer in time, that the bus would hurtle forward into the unknown, into some part of town that was foreign to me, and that I wouldn't know how to get back, each time I sat anxiously in the front of the bus, my little hands tightly grasping the chromium handrail as I looked ahead for the landmarks that never seemed to become familiar.

My mother must have recognized my fear; it must have been plain on my face, because at that age I couldn't have been adept at concealing it. But she left me alone to weather it, and maybe because she did, I was able to make those more extensive journeys later as an adult.

Even when I arrived in the kindergarten room in the basement of the school, things weren't any better. I was no better equipped at age six than I am now to walk into a room full of strangers and feel at ease. So I never willingly joined the other children in the projects around the tables, painting with tempera or making chains out of strips of paper. There was a little rocking chair in the room, and I preferred to be there by myself, joining the others only when urged, and then uncomfortably.

It was an inauspicious introduction to the world outside our home and neighborhood. So when that long year was over and I could start real school in the fall of 1945, I was eager—not to read and write and work with numbers but to spend more time with my neighborhood friends and escape the heavy hands of boredom and loneliness.

5

...the self is not something that one finds.
It is something that one creates.

The Second Sin—
Thomas Szaz

Growing up, that ragged, discomforting enterprise, that haphazard series of lurches and sputters and leaps, often begins with the sudden awareness that other families are different from our families, that other people are not like us.

For me, the process took a great leap with that glimpse and sniff of the interior world of Mrs. Dennison, and Roosevelt Elementary School picked up from there. A four-story, maroon brick building shaped like a slightly flattened cube, it had opened in 1910, and when I started school there in the fall of 1945, its wood floors, its classroom radiators where we put our mittens to dry, its old wooden desks with holes for long-ago inkwells, its chalkboards with the letters of the alphabet, upper and lower case, in the correct, Palmer method, all had the whiff of a bygone era.

When I started first grade I tended toward the scrawny and, having had to sit out the previous year, was advantageously taller than my classmates. I had short brown hair with a cowlick in front, crooked teeth that would later be straightened by braces, and a heavily freckled face. It was the freckles that bothered me. "Where'd you get all those freckles?" adults would ask, a question that even then struck me as stupid. In photos and 8mm home movies from those years, I'm rarely smiling.

Normally my neighborhood friends and I walked the mile to school, even in winter when we'd pull on our black, buckle overshoes, wool jackets, wool stocking caps, and woolen mittens with the leather shells, then follow the snow-packed streets. You knew it was cold when the snow squeaked underfoot, or when Pop gave us a ride, which he did when the mercury dropped to 15 or 20 below.

At the time, I didn't appreciate how lucky I was that the classroom part of my education was easy for me. I could zip through passages in Dick and Jane while others stumbled over words with agonizing uncertainty; I was among the last ones standing in spelling bees; I could do arithmetic problems on the blackboard, then return to my seat and wait impatiently for those who needed help from the teacher. Even though I sensed the embarrassment of children who knew they were slowing down the class—could see it in their flushed faces and in the sweaty palms they wiped nervously on their corduroy trousers or woolen skirts—I certainly didn't sympathize with them. Oblivious to the fact that whatever ability I had stemmed not from my own efforts but from the accident of birth, instead I reveled obnoxiously in the feeling of superiority and resented them for holding the rest of us back.

In music we sang nineteenth century folk songs like "Blue Tail Fly" and "She'll be Comin' Round the Mountain When She Comes," and some Stephen Foster—"Beautiful Dreamer," "Camptown Races," "Oh! Susanna," and "I Dream of Jeannie With the Light Brown Hair." Why school children in mid-twentieth century North Dakota should sing antiquated songs about the sun shining bright on old Kentucky homes, about darkies being gay, about young folks rolling on the little cabin floor is baffling to me now, but it's even more baffling to think that we sang a song like "Old Folks at Home."

> *Way down upon de Swannee ribber,*
> *Far, far away,*
> *Dere's wha my heart is turning ebber,*
> *Dere's wha de old folks stay.*

> *All up and down the whole creation,*
> *Sadly I roam,*
> *Still longing for the old plantation,*
> *And for the old folks at home.*

> *All the world is sad and dreary,*
> *Ebry where I roam,*
> *Oh! Darkeys how my heart grows weary,*
> *Far from de old folks at home.*

Still six years away from the start of racial integration in the public schools and more than a decade away from the first rumblings of the civil rights movement, we sang that dreary song in our cheerful, pre-adolescent voices and never gave a thought to its inappropriateness in our particular place and time. It doesn't seem likely that our teachers intended us to ponder the world view of slaves in the pre

Civil War South; where race was concerned, they were probably no more aware than their students.

In gym class we often played Pursuit Race, a game with lessons more profound and more indelible than any I learned in the classroom. I learned that I was a fast runner, one of the fastest in our class, a discovery that became the cornerstone of the identity I'd create for myself and later cultivate vigorously for the rest of my school days. And I saw the hard-heartedness of the faster runners who didn't conceal disgust with the slower ones, usually girls, who caused our team to lose and who must have dreaded that game as much as I relished it.

At Roosevelt I brushed against children who seemed to be from other worlds, who appeared as exotic to me then as some foreigners seem today. One of them, Robert Sawatsky, a pale, quiet, dark-haired boy with a soft, apologetic smile, lived west of Washington Avenue, an area of unpaved streets and small, unkempt houses with unkempt yards. From my little world, everything west of Washington Avenue was not just the other side of the tracks but an alien land.

We sat in alphabetical order in class, so I was always in the back of the room, always one seat behind Robert. One day in class as I was studying the back of Robert's head, I watched a small insect crawl out of his matted, unwashed hair and disappear under the collar of his plaid flannel shirt; and I realized then that the seemingly familiar boy who had been sitting directly in front of me for several years was as different from me as anyone I could then imagine. Suddenly, in one of those lurches of awareness, I knew something I had never known before: As I sat there freshly washed, in clean clothes, as I thought about our large house on Lincoln Drive and our up-to-date car and our long, grassy lawn flowing down to the river, I knew that if I had ever been cruel to Robert Sawatsky before, it would be much harder to be cruel to him again.

In fifth grade when we had to memorize a poem and recite it in class, I chose Oliver Wendell Holmes' "Old Ironsides." Or, more likely, someone—Mom, say, or our teacher—chose it for me. After my classroom recitation, I realized that this had been a contest, that I'd won, and that my reward was to recite the poem again from the stage at an all-school assembly, which looked to me less like a reward than a punishment. But as an obedient child I wouldn't have thought to decline, wouldn't have dared say, "Thanks, but I prefer not to," so I just went ahead with it, utterly without satisfaction or pride. Even then there were signs that unlike my Grandfather McIntosh I'd never make a name for myself as an orator.

In that most instructive class called Recess, it was more difficult for me to fit in. The stars at Recess were usually not the ones who shone in the classrooms indoors but the ones who tried to be inconspicuous, the ones who stumbled over numbers and words, who said "He don't" and "I ain't"—boys like Charlie Novak and Duce Haugen. In the classroom you barely knew they were there, but outdoors at recess they became dauntless and brash. In winter when we played King of the Hill on large mounds of snow piled high by the plows, it was usually Charlie or Duce who ended up on top. In spring or fall, the game was marbles—a game we didn't play in our Lincoln Drive neighborhood—and Charlie and Duce called the shots. They carried large collections of marbles in cloth bags and they spoke a language of their own, using words like "crockies," "puries," and "steelies," and expressions like "rounds, fan pays" or "knuckles down, screw baloney." For some of those boys, marbles had a strong allure: There was a national marbles competition then, and more than once a boy from Grand Forks became national champion. I'd have to make my name some other way.

◆   ◆   ◆

During the 1949-50 school year, when I was in the fifth grade and one of my favorite articles of clothing was a bow tie with little light bulbs I could flash on and off with a battery in my pocket, momentous events were taking place in the world. The Communists took over China, the USSR detonated its first atomic bomb and the nuclear arms race began, the North Korean Communists crossed the 38th Parallel to begin the Korean War, and Senator Joseph McCarthy was fanning the fear of Communism here at home. The Department of Defense released a 438-page report on how to survive a nuclear attack. (Remain in your bomb shelter for two to four hours, it said, then wash thoroughly. Don't beget offspring for two to three months.) And Dr. Alfred Kinsey published *Sexual Behavior of the Human Male*, a shocking book based on interviews with 5,300 white men. (Police tried to interfere with the questioning, which covered topics such as the frequency of orgasm, masturbation, oral sex, petting, and marital and extramarital intercourse, and later hindered the publication of the book. Some libraries wouldn't put it on the shelves.)

Mahatma Gandhi had just been assassinated in India, the Communists had recently taken over Czechoslovakia, Israel had just been founded, and President Truman ended racial discrimination in the U.S. military services.

But I knew only about the important things—the opening of a new elementary school in the south end of town just two blocks from our house. When we transferred to this brand new building in the winter of the 1949-50, it wasn't quite finished. Scraps of lumber, short lengths of conduit and electrical wire, and pieces of pipe still littered the grounds, and in the classrooms, wires still stuck out of the walls where clocks would be. Everything was spotless—the desk tops and green chalkboards were unmarked, the walls were clean, the tile floors were shiny—and we had the exhilarating feeling of being in on something exciting and new.

One winter morning at that brand new school, I put on my jacket and woolen mittens and walked outside for recess, and as I was standing outdoors in the cold, watching my breath, stamping my feet to keep warm, and wondering what to do with myself, I picked up a 10-inch piece of galvanized pipe and began twirling it around my head before throwing it into the street. It was a cold winter morning so there was frost on the pipe, and I was wearing woolen mittens so the pipe stuck to the wool, and when I opened my fingers to release it, the pipe stuck to my mitten for just a moment too long, and rather than follow its intended course toward the street, the pipe flew instead through a brand new window of the brand new school.

The double pane window broken by the errant pipe was not just any school window; it was the principal's window, and as always the principal was there at his post.

In a stunningly short time I was seated across the desk from the scariest man I had ever seen, a man who we all knew kept a rubber hose in his bottom drawer. Mr. Loomer was disconcertingly gaunt, with hollow cheeks and sunken eyes and a slit-like mouth that was several degrees off the horizontal. Leaning forward, his arms crossed on his desk in front of him, he peered into my skull. It might have been easier had he pounded his desk and railed at me for my stupidity, or gotten out the rubber hose, but he didn't. He just sat there quietly and stared at me.

The facts of the case weren't in dispute. From his office window he'd seen me throw the pipe and had watched the pipe sail through the double-paned glass. There was only the question of what should happen next.

It was obvious the window had to be fixed—Mr. Loomer and I sat shivering as the winter wind poured through the broken pane—but at whose expense? Mr. Loomer certainly hadn't caused the damage; he shouldn't have to pay for it, we agreed. My parents hadn't done it either; no one—not even I—could see any reason *they* should have to pay. That left, alas, me. I agreed to cover the damage—$40—with money I'd earn through my own labors. It was sort of a plea bargain, I guess, and it spared me the rubber hose.

There was no finger-wagging on Mr. Loomer's part, no lengthy sermon or admonition. It was a pretty straightforward transaction based on our mutual recognition that what was broken ought to be made whole, that what was wrong ought to be made right. There might have been some behind-the-scenes collaboration between Mr. Loomer and my parents in the disposition of the case—that was how things worked back then—but if there were I never knew of it. I knew only that long after the event Mr. Loomer, this man I regarded with fear and dread, this man with the rubber hose in his desk drawer, was enigmatically still "a dear" in my mother's eyes.

There was a similar outcome the next year when I brought a pocketknife to school and carved my name into the wooden seat of my desk. Mr. Volker, my first male teacher, a tall, muscular, athletic-looking man with a short crew cut and a long, sharp nose, was not impressed with my handiwork. Like Mr. Loomer, he didn't storm and shout; he simply kept me after school one day and wordlessly handed me a piece of sandpaper and a sanding block. The jig being up—I didn't have to ask how he knew it was me—I got down on my knees on the hard tile floor and discovered that sanding hardwood is even more laborious than carving it.

In spite of what these stories reveal about my intelligence at age 12, I tell them for what they reveal about school discipline in that long-ago time before the erosion of personal responsibility, before intervention by parents and lawyers and courts and the Civil Liberties Union. (As Ovid said, it's annoying to be honest to no purpose.) These experiences led to the realization that erasing all evidence of my crimes by my own labors was surprisingly satisfying. Paying for my own stupidities allowed me to be on good terms with Mr. Loomer and Mr. Volker again and helped to abate the ever-present fear of the rubber hose.

◆　　　◆　　　◆

When my classmates and I became sixth graders and ruled the school, we were unbeatable on the athletic field. I was captain of the touch football team that fall—or quarterback, I'm not sure I knew the difference—a position I attained less by any demonstrable capacity to lead than by being a little older and still a little bit taller than most of my teammates. It wouldn't be the last time my classmates looked to me for leadership, but maybe it should have been: I didn't have a very good instinct for calling plays, and when the official called a penalty on the opposing team and asked me if I wanted fourth and one or third and 11, I was easily flustered and never sure I was making the right decision.

But we had a speedy runner named "By" Evenson whom no one in the city could catch, and we had two tall ends—"Bear" Grinnell and Armin Hughes, who had an after school job setting pins at the Uptown bowling alley and who had a girlfriend named Rita whose name he inscribed in ballpoint pen on the back of his hand, drawing a heart around it and an arrow through the heart. Bear and Armin towered above defenders and had no trouble pulling in passes.

When we came up against Winship from the north end of town, we were warned we might have our hands full. Their star running back, Marvin Kosmatka, was a terror, we heard; he'd run wild over us.

In their first possession, the Winship quarterback called for a run around their right end and flipped the ball to the dreaded Marvin Kosmatka. "Oh oh," I thought, "we're in for it now." But by the time Marvin got to the line of scrimmage he found a gang of our—our what? I can't call them tacklers, since this was touch football. Our touchers?—he found a gang of our touchers lying in wait for him. His bespectacled face flooded with dismay, he stopped abruptly in his tracks and, rather than be caught with the football, he did what I'd never seen before and have never seen since: He just coughed the ball straight up into the air, as if to say, "It's not my problem anymore." We won the game easily, as we did all the others, and we went on to be named city champions with our picture in the paper. It was pretty hot stuff. (I didn't see Marvin again until high school, when we were teammates in junior varsity football. When he took off his helmet one day at practice, I noticed that he inexplicably carried inside the lining a glossary of ore-bearing rocks.)

We had comparable success in basketball, no thanks to me. My instinct in basketball, like my instinct in some other pursuits, was to be in the thin of the action, to participate from the perimeter, to get rid of the ball as soon as I could, feeding it to teammates who knew what to do with it. But the discomfort I felt because of my mediocrity was outweighed by the reassuring feeling of being on the team, of being one of the gang, and of being city champions in another sport.

I liked track better, because it was an individual sport and because I could capitalize on the speed I'd discovered a few years earlier at Roosevelt. Even if I'd known I'd set a city record in the long jump in sixth grade—a fact I didn't learn until years later—I couldn't have liked the sport any more. I just liked to run; I could do it for a long time without getting tired, and I liked putting my body to that kind of test. Somehow we just *know* when we've found a pursuit that accommodates our temperament and our abilities, and even though I couldn't have put it into words at the time, I sensed at age 12 that I had found mine. Already showing some of my father's reticence, at least in running I could express myself in another way. Besides, an individual sport accommodated my incipient, stubborn resolution to succeed or fail on my own terms. With running, my childhood was starting to take an agreeable direction.

Not content with our accomplishments, we use them as fuel for dreams in which we're always bigger, stronger, more accomplished than we really are, as groundwork for a fantasy in which not only our talents but their results are magnified beyond reason, beyond the power of reality to sustain. But such is the mind of a child, and such is the unpredictable, haphazard business of creating a self.

It was while I was in elementary school and trying to establish myself as an athletic hero that Mom and Pop decided to inflict music lessons on Paul and me. Mom had been raised with music around her and remembered how much benefit she had derived from singing and playing the piano, and I suspect that in some wild flight of fancy she envisioned those same kinds of benefits accruing to her children. It was all in accord with one of the most acclaimed goals of the era—to be "well rounded." A widely published magazine ad for piano instruction showed a handsome, well groomed young man at the keyboard, surrounded by adoring fans. "They may laugh when you sit down at the piano," the ad said, "but wait 'til they hear you play." Like so many parents, Mom was in for a disappointment

Paul, unfortunately for the rest of the family, chose the violin. He sawed away on that poor instrument to the acute discomfort of the rest of the household, and when in a short time he was allowed to retire from his brief violin career on the reasonable assumption that his talents lay elsewhere, it was as if a curse had suddenly been lifted.

I chose the piano, starting with John Thompson's Book Number One with its red cover. At that point I wasn't amenable to tasks that called for mental discipline or for sitting in one place for more than a few minutes at a time. And I didn't like going to Mrs. Bustyn's for lessons after school: Her house was filled with China figurines and doily-covered furniture; when she led me across the living room to the piano bench, her nylons made swishing sounds as she walked; and when she sat down next to me on the bench, her excess of perfume made me woozy.

After a couple of years with the piano, in probably the most uncharacteristic, most daring act of my life to date, I told Mom I wanted to quit. She couldn't have been completely surprised; as a piano player herself, she wouldn't have been blind to my marginal aptitude or my foot-dragging approach to practice. She tried to deflect me from my course: "If you're going to quit," she said, "you'll have to tell Mrs. Bustyn yourself."

Her strategy was transparent to me even then: I wouldn't have the nerve to tell Mrs. Bustyn myself so I'd go on with the piano by default. But all I needed was the challenge, and in responding to it I taught my mother never to doubt my resolve. I made the call to Mrs. Bustyn, retired from my career as a pianist, and—with a new and exploding sense of life's possibilities—returned to my friends and the playground, inhaling the cool, fresh air of liberation, exhilarated by the useful discovery that resolution pays.

◆   ◆   ◆

When I look back on my childhood today, it's surprising to realize that I was 12 years old before I got into my first and only fight. My opponent was Billy Paradise, a boy I feared because of his resemblance to Sluggo in the "Nancy" comic strip; he had a round head with close-cut hair, rounded shoulders, a surly demeanor, and a gravelly voice even though he was only 12. He shuffled when he walked, and the hands that he thrust in his pockets always looked like they were curled into fists.

I don't remember how it began, but Billy and I wrestled around for a while in the playground dirt, grunting and puffing, and eventually, to my amazement, I ended up on top. What I remember most about this landmark of my childhood is his cry of frustration when he went limp and gave up the fight: "You rich guys think you're so tough."

Well, now, *there* was something to think about. It seems that I was about to experience another of those sudden lurches of discovery. I'd never thought of myself as tough, even though I'd held my own in my fights with Paul. And even though I *had* just beaten up this hitherto dreaded Sluggo look-alike with the gravelly voice, all my instincts pushed me away from confrontations, and I doubted if anyone considered me tough.

"Rich" was a little more complicated. I'd been vaguely aware that I had some advantages others didn't—that we had a much bigger house and a newer car than some of my friends, that I had nicer clothes, that I knew better than to say "I ain't" and "he don't." I was aware that most other children weren't able to walk into stores downtown and charge things to their parents and that most of them didn't have summer vacation homes or memberships in the country club. But even though I'd sensed all this and was a little uneasy about it, until my fight with Billy Paradise I hadn't put this feeling into words.

It was Billy Paradise who unwittingly helped to sharpen my awareness of my place in our small social world, or at least my place as *he* saw it, and to let me know that some people, or at least one, resented me for it. I didn't *want* to be resented—even by Billy Paradise—so, not wanting enemies, not wanting to be thought rich—meaning *different*—I did what I could to downplay my advantages and be one of the gang.

Another unwitting teacher in this field of study, a classmate named Larry Rosenthal, lived in one of the small houses on lower Lincoln Drive where families often had to abandon their homes in the spring and retreat from the Red River floods. Wherever Larry is today, I'm sure he would be flabbergasted to hear that I envied him and his parents for raising chickens in their backyard. What fun, I thought, to have a yard full of chickens. Then this thought: If Larry and his parents could raise a handful of chickens in *their* small yard, think of the number of chickens *we* could raise in our long backyard that flowed 100 yards down the hill to the river. With a backyard the size of ours, there was no sensible reason *not* to raise chickens. But my parents were no more interested in keeping chickens than Pop had been in quitting medicine to become a coal man. Another good idea was squashed. Their stance seemed unimaginative and unreasonable, and my simmering disappointment might have been avoided had they explained what took me so much longer to understand on my own—that the Rosenthals didn't raise chickens for fun.

Social and economic differences were a troublesome thicket to navigate. We like to pretend they don't exist, that we're all one, cozy, egalitarian family, that one man is the same as another. And in many ways, where I grew up it's true. No one ever told me directly or indirectly to play with children of our own kind, to stay away from children who had less than we had or to look up to those who had more. Still, sooner or later we sense that there *are* differences, that some people have bigger houses and cars than others, and nicer clothes, that some children have rotten teeth and don't bathe very often and use bad language. These differences puzzle us and make us uncomfortable, but we're too polite to talk about them; they don't fit neatly with our egalitarian ideal. So we go on as if they aren't there, getting no guidance in this business when we're young, muddling through these complexities in ignorance, finally bumbling into awareness through the haphazard teacher called experience.

◆   ◆   ◆

Of all the delicious experiences of childhood, one of the best is waking up on the first day of summer vacation and remembering that three months of freedom are spread out ahead of you. Lying in the upper bunk above Paul (Don had a room of his own)—my plastic model airplanes suspended from the ceiling above me, I'd slowly rise to the level of consciousness, drawing out the experience as long as I could, allowing the luxurious feeling of freedom to wash over me. I lay there listening to the robins singing in the tops of the elms and the mourning doves cooing from the blue spruce in Mrs. Dennison's front yard, delighting in the prospect of three whole unscheduled months ahead. Earlier, in that long, burdensome year before first grade, time had been an unwelcome guest; now, on the first day of summer vacation, it was an opportunity, a gift, especially once Mom and Pop decided we were old enough to play by the river.

When summer vacation began, the boys in the neighborhood—there were about a dozen of us, with about four or five years difference in age between the youngest (me) and the oldest—headed down the hill toward the river to revel in three months of adventure. (I know as historical fact that there were two girls in the neighborhood, but they hadn't burst into my consciousness yet.)

The major players in the summer drama:

Jerry Loft—thin, with straight brown hair and thick glasses. On our earliest association, Jerry and I dressed up as cowboys, wearing cowboy hats and chaps, bandanas around our necks, and six shooter cap guns in our holsters. To extend the image we tried rolling our own cigarettes using wide line notebook paper and dried leaves, but when we lit them we singed our lips.

David Ray—with straw colored hair, round red cheeks, a bashful smile, and a farm-kid look about him. He was one of those people who pronounce "wash" as "warsh." To Dave, the capitol of our nation was Warshington, DC, and our first president was George Warshington. We tried futilely to convince him otherwise.

Dave Hulteng—stocky, square-headed, and pigeon-toed. Dave had a funny laugh that sounded like a squirrel chattering. He preferred to walk with his hands in his back pockets. It was his parents who conceived the hoolihookoos.

Bill Bonhoff—tall, slender, brown-haired, known around the neighborhood as an "only child," a term often uttered then in the same tone of voice one might use in saying "orphan." Bill, inappropriately serious and self-righteous, had an inexhaustible capacity for indignation. When seized by one of those fits in the middle of a game, he predictably threatened to go home and take the ball with him.

Jerry Nehring—bespectacled, taller than Bill, tall enough to be nicknamed "Highpockets." Jerry was also an only child. We played Kick the Can in the alley behind his house and used his single car garage for our games of Anti-I-Over. The garage had a loft we used as a hideout. Jerry once blew up the end of a finger with firecrackers.

The Hanson brothers, Dick and Bob—like Bill, approached our childhood play with undue seriousness. In our neighborhood we all addressed each other by our last names. Jerry Nehring was "Nehring," Bill Bonhoff was "Bonhoff," and so on. (I was "Little Woutat, to distinguish me from Paul.) The Hansons, following suit, even addressed one another as "Hanson."

The Grinnell brothers—Dave, whom we called "Noodle," and his younger brother Paul, whom we called "Bear"—dark-haired, good at neighborhood sports, with eyes of the kind that girls die for. Ironically, the older brother Dave was shorter than the younger brother Paul, so "Little Grinnell" was actually taller than "Big Grinnell."

In our earliest summers along the river our pleasures were simple, starting with our invention of mud slingers. We cut thin, 18-inch switches of green willow and stuck walnuts of mud on the end, then—using little more than a flick of the wrist—discovered that with this simple tool we could propel those little wads amazing distances. We could never have thrown a stone across the river—it was too wide—but with the mud slingers we could easily flick little wads of North Dakota soil clear into another state.

We didn't spend much time fishing because there wasn't much to catch but bullheads, loathsome-looking fish with stingers that make it tough to get out the hook. My solution was to hold the fish down with my foot so I wouldn't have to see him or touch him, then grip the line tightly and yank the hook out—sometimes insides came out with it—then kick the dead fish back into the river and watch it float lazily downstream. I was repulsed by its lifeless, pale yellow belly, but at the same time sorry I'd killed it.

It was more fun to fish with explosives. Even as children we could get our hands on dangerous fireworks—sky rockets, pinwheels, firecrackers, and a much more powerful explosive called a G-Whiz, a thick, stubby firecracker about the size of a cigar butt with a waterproof fuse sticking out from the side. These babies had punch. Today they're probably restricted to munitions experts, but as children we could simply order them through the mail. In our backyard was an open metal pipe embedded in a small concrete slab where Mom used to erect the post for her portable clothesline. When we lighted a G-Whiz, dropped it into the pipe, and placed a tennis ball on top, the blast shot the ball almost out of sight.

It was the G-Whiz that became part of our fishing tackle. After lighting the waterproof fuse, we tossed it into the river and waited expectantly while it slowly worked its way toward the bottom. Eventually we heard a *whump*, then saw a little mound of water appear for a moment on the surface. Sometimes a dead bullhead or two would rise to the top and we'd cheer as they drifted lazily away with the current. It was a more dramatic form of fishing, and it was easier and less repulsive than jerking out hooks.

When we ran out of G-Whiz, we fed our need for noise and destruction with homemade devices. The ingredients were simple: copper pipe we'd bought at the hardware store and shotgun shells we'd stolen from Pop's gun closet. We crimped one end of the pipe, filled the tube with gunpowder from the shotgun shells, then crimped the other end. We poked a hole in the side with a small nail and inserted a firecracker fuse. For maximum commotion, we dropped these crude explosives into an empty, metal garbage can and quickly replaced the lid. Some of those garbage cans blew apart at the seams, but the noise was wonderfully gratifying.

One summer we began our most ambitious riverside project of all. It started at the Army/Navy surplus store, one of my favorite places in town with its distinctive Army/Navy surplus smell, with the inflated, yellow life rafts suspended from the ceiling and its inventory of mess kits, fatigue pants, camouflage clothing, canvas pup tents, ammunition boxes, and machetes, all in olive drab, and where for a couple of dollars each, we bought Army "entrenching tools," the small shovels with blades that fold back against the handle. Armed with these tools, the neighborhood gang charged down the grassy hill toward the river, toward a venture that impresses me still.

In the tall grass amid the giant cottonwoods, we chose a site about thirty yards from the river's edge and began to dig. If we'd been 10 years older, we might have been using those same tools to dig foxholes in Korea while artillery exploded around us, but in the mindless years of childhood we were free of such concerns. With those little shovels—not much bigger, it seemed, than soupspoons—it took a long time; but the digging itself wasn't difficult because the deep black earth was soft and damp. When we were through we had a hole about four feet deep and eight feet square. The earth had the texture of cheddar cheese, so we were able to shave the walls straight and the corners square and to carve cool, damp earthen benches along the sides. We found scrap lumber and tree branches to put over the top, then covered those with scraps of cardboard, then a layer of leftover dirt, leaving a hole in one corner for the entrance. For illumination we first used candles mounted in niches carved in the walls, but eventually one of the Hulteng brothers brought in a dry cell, some electrical wire, and a flashlight bulb, and with these simple materials, in an act of wizardry that dazzled us all, he suddenly propelled our Stone Age cave into the age of electricity.

We spent a lot of time in the cave that summer. It brought us together because so many of us had shared in the digging. We liked it because we'd carved it out of the earth with our own hands, because it was private, beyond the intruding eyes of adults, because we could meet there to read dirty joke books the older boys had filched from Widmer's drugstore and to smoke cigarettes we'd stolen from home.

(Heedless of early reports from scientists that smoking might cause cancer, we were hell-bent on giving tobacco a try, suspecting with Fran Liebowitz that smoking is the entire point of being an adult. We agreed that cigarettes didn't taste very good so we went to Woolworth's to buy corncob pipes that were in keeping with our Huck Finn, riverside style, and in those pipes we tried smoking just about anything that burned—cigarette tobacco, dried leaves, coffee grounds, and corn silk. Eventually, feeling we'd given it a fair shake, we decided that smoking wasn't what it was cracked up to be and we retired from it, at least for the time being.)

The next spring we learned the perils of owning your own home by the Red River. When the river rose out of its banks, our cave was under water for weeks, and when the water finally subsided our summer retreat was almost obliterated: The high water had carried off the lumber-and-cardboard roof and left the hole almost filled with greasy, gray mud that took weeks to dry.

But when the river was finally back in its banks and the earth was dry again, we dug out the cave to its original shape, found more scrap lumber and cardboard to rebuild the roof, and moved back in for the summer. Like families downstream who were scooping mud from their basements and living rooms, like families everywhere who have been uprooted by floods or famines or marauding tribes, we were, in our childish way, following an ancient pattern: We were obeying the fundamental instinct to rebuild, to settle again, to regain what we'd lost. We spent as much time as we could in the renovation because we'd already learned that the pleasure was in the doing. Once the job was done, there really wasn't very much to do underground; smoking having lost its appeal, there wasn't much left but trading comic books. Superman, Batman, Plastic Man, and Spiderman were the best.

Our river world was mostly a boys' world; I never saw a girl there and rarely saw a man. Sometimes a man would appear, usually alone and unkempt, usually walking suspiciously along the dirt road by the golf course when men should have been at work. One was a shaggy young man in an undershirt who ambled to the riverbank one hot summer weekday afternoon, stripped to his underwear, and dove into the river to swim. It was a shocking sight—the first time I'd ever seen anyone actually go into that muddy, intimidating river—but he did it, and he came out safely, and in the process he unwittingly destroyed the neighborhood myth about the terrible undertow and the hoolihookoos.

The only other adult visitor to our riverside world was a regular, Frank Kovnick, an old man who lived two blocks away on Lanark and who spent many summer days alone by the river where he sat on the ground, leaning against the red brick pump house and carving little canoes out of cottonwood bark. No matter how warm the weather, he dressed in a fresh, white, long-sleeved shirt buttoned up to the neck, with black elastic armbands above the elbows, and a straw hat. One day when I was alone I worked up enough nerve to approach him. He held out a little canoe he had just finished, and after pausing a moment I took it from his thick, callused fingers. Neither of us spoke. As I walked away, I examined the little wooden vessel about three inches long. It was amazingly light in my hand. I never recognized that boat as a gesture, and I never thanked him for it because in the thoughtlessness of childhood, it never occurred to me. Nor did it occur to my little friends and me to wonder why an old man would spend so much time alone by the river, to realize that he might be lonely, that he might have nothing to fill his days but carve little boats and watch the river go by. So it doesn't surprise me now that my little friends and I could storm through his yard on our bikes in the evening and snatch apples from his trees, and when he came out of his house to protest, that we could laugh at his helplessness.

These subterranean summers were the same summers we fought our rubber gun wars. The "bullet" fired from these guns was a heavy duty rubber band, a cross section of a car inner tube cut to a one-inch width. The "gun" itself we built from scraps of one-by-twos, an 18-inch section for the barrel and a six-inch piece attached at about a 45-degree angle for a pistol grip. One end of the "rubber band" was looped over the muzzle end of the gun and the other was stretched back toward the opposite end of the barrel where it was held in place by a spring clothespin attached to the pistol grip. For more firepower you made a longer barrel and, for the projectile, cross sections of a truck inner tube.

When we got a little older, some of us got BB guns. Mine was a Red Ryder lever action that fired copper-colored BB's with enough power to kill small birds. With my Red Ryder lever action I became Daniel Boone—one of my heroes then—creeping stealthily through the trees by the river, stalking Indians, or being stalked. At one point, impatient with make-believe, we started firing at each other, hiding in the tall grass beneath the cottonwoods, darting up quickly to squeeze off another shot at the enemy's head, then ducking for cover again in the grass. It certainly hurt to be hit by one of those BB's, but there was no danger in it, we thought. Sometimes a BB broke the skin and disappeared underneath, but if you just squeezed it like a pimple it popped right out. As Mark Twain said, "Providence protects children and idiots. I know because I have tested it."

We played the more usual childhood games too—Kick the Can, Hide and Seek, Anti-I-Over, Statues, Crack and Whip, Red Rover—games that were familiar all over the country. (Years later a colleague told me she'd played many of those same games as a child in Scotland.) But as I observe neighborhood children today from my living room window, I don't see them playing these kinds of games. Once in a while they play catch or shoot baskets at the hoop my neighbor put up, but mostly they're indoors watching television or videos and surfing the Net.

It's as if my generation grew up in a different country from theirs. Our generation may have been the last to grow up in two-parent households in which all fathers worked and all mothers were at home with their children. Ours was the last generation to enjoy a childhood free from the great mesmerizer, television. Our childhood may be the last to be free of illicit drugs, drive-by shootings, and guns in schools. With no violence around us, there was no need for institutionalized play in the form of tennis lessons and ballet lessons to preoccupy us and shield us from harm. We had no X-rated movies to tantalize us, no Internet pornography seeping into our homes, no open discussion about oral sex to puzzle and confuse us. Today, the best we can do is long for that kind of world.

◆　　◆　　◆

It was great fortune to have a river in our backyard; but on top of that we also had five crab apple trees in our neighborhood—three at the Thorgrimsons and two at the Hoghaugs, new neighbors who'd replaced the Hultengs—and by August, when the apples were fully formed—the size of walnuts or ping pong balls—they were the perfect size for throwing at cars. With the Rays at their farm home for the summer, their flat-roofed house across the street from ours was vacant, so in the evenings, our pockets filled with crab apples, we borrowed their wooden ladder, climbed to their roof, and pulled the ladder up behind us. Around the perimeter of the roof was a wall just high enough to conceal us, so we crouched behind the wall and waited for passing cars. As a car drove by, we pelted it with crab apples, delighting in the *bonk* when they hit the hood or the roof, then ducked behind the wall. One night a driver screeched to a halt and ran toward the house to catch us. Peaking over the wall above him, barely muffling our amusement, we watched as he searched for us in the shrubs below, muttering and swearing and finally returning to his car and peeling away.

One night we filled our pockets with crab apples and headed across the golf course to Belmont Road. Crouching behind bushes, we listened for approaching cars, then rose up and fired. Sometimes the crab apples were already in the air by the time we actually saw our target. If that happens often enough, we learned, the odds are that the vehicle you hit will be the one you least want to hit. The police car screeched to a stop, the door flew open, and we began our sprint in the opposite direction, soon passing beyond the range of the streetlight into the safe, silent darkness of the golf course. "Stop or I'll shoot," the policeman yelled, but we didn't. We sprinted across five fairways and through Lincoln Park, then one more block to our house. The garage door was open so we ran inside and waited in the dark to catch our breath. We were safe now, we thought, so we left the garage door open.

Minutes later the police car pulled into our driveway, its headlights pinning us to the garage wall, and inside with the policeman was one of our accomplices, Tommy Hoghaug, who greeted us from the inside of the police car with a smile and a cheery wave. He'd stopped on the policeman's command, he confessed later, and—not yet having developed a knack for making new friends—led the officer straight to our house. The next morning, the officer said, we had an appointment downtown at the station. "You may have some jail time ahead of you," he said with a straight face.

The next morning, we crab apple criminals convened on the Lincoln Drive bus and rode downtown to our destiny at the Grand Forks Police Station, utterly unprotected by our parents or a battalion of lawyers. We were ushered solemnly into the police matron's office where, over an uncomfortably long time, we were given "a good talking-to," as adults used to say in those days; but her exact words were obliterated by the heavy fear of imprisonment. Finally, nervously, one of us put the question: "Wwwwill we have to go to jail?" She considered the question with a studied frown. "No," she finally answered. "Not this time." She then uttered the immortal words that over the generations have saved so many children from lives of crime: "But this will go on your permanent record." We believed in the "permanent record" as fervently as we'd once believed in the hoolihookoos and the rubber hose, and we never threw anything at cars again.

Another illustration of contemporary justice was delivered by Dr. Hoghaug, Tommy's father. Because Tommy was a new kid in the neighborhood, it seemed appropriate to my neighborhood friends and me that we subject him to unrelenting torment, which one winter afternoon took the form of an assault by snowballs. It was probably poor strategy on our part that we executed this assault in his own yard, where his own father could see us. He burst from his door in anger and we took flight in fear. In spite of the cold, he hadn't taken time to put on a coat and, still wearing bedroom slippers, he gave chase through the snow. We sprinted across the street toward our house, then raced down the hill toward the river, the be-slippered, middle-aged Dr. Hoghaug in hot pursuit.

He had more speed than we might have given him credit for. At the bottom of the hill he caught up with us and, as they used to say in the crime stories, the jig was up. He might have dragged us up the hill by our coat collars and ranted and railed at us in front of our parents, but he didn't. His approach was more like Mr. Loomer's. And that was enough. We didn't throw snowballs at Tommy again.

If our parents witnessed this little demonstration of curbside justice from their picture window at the top of the hill, they never said so. They wouldn't have. They could see that Dr. Hoghaug had things in hand, and they could rightly assume that we deserved whatever it was we were getting. That's just how things worked those days.

But there were plenty of other ways to amuse ourselves. We gathered at the top of the hill at Lincoln Park and chose up sides for softball or baseball or played a game of 500, and in the fall when we got bored with baseball we took up football, playing either tackle or touch. When we played tackle we all put on shoulder pads, not because we played hard enough to damage each other but because they made us look monstrous and intimidating. I loved putting on the pads and tugging a sweatshirt over them, then marveling at my brawn in the full-length mirror. Anyone wearing something as sensible as a helmet would have been ridiculed.

In those reckless, thoughtless years of childhood, the dangers we imposed on ourselves with our homemade explosives and our BB gun wars were real, but we faced a far greater danger in the most frightening disease of the time—polio. The more benign childhood illnesses—chicken pox, mumps, measles, even though they were annoying and sometimes called for quarantine—were short-term events. And the ringworm epidemic of my grade school years—which at worst caused temporary baldness and required that for several months we all wear little white cotton skull caps at school and in public places like movie theaters—ring-worm too was little more than an inconvenience. But polio was serious business.

Not that we children lost sleep over it, we children who were immune to injury and death. It *was* a worry to our parents, though, because the polio virus—which affected mostly children and young adults—could result in atrophy to the skeletal muscles, physical deformity, or deterioration of the respiratory muscles, which meant a life sentence in an iron lung. Other forms of the virus made it difficult to speak and eat. All of which explains my mother's reaction the day I accidentally inhaled the sulphuric wisps of smoke from my cap gun and began gasping for breath. Her face was instantly flooded with horror, and in the minute or two before I could speak again and put her at ease, she probably saw an iron lung in my future and nothing else. Until the polio vaccine was developed in 1953, our parents lived with that kind of fear.

◆   ◆   ◆

When I was 10, I developed an urge to upgrade my transportation from an ordinary, nondescript bicycle to a heavy Schwinn, non-gear, fat-tired bike with a large leather seat and a suspension system over the front fork to soften the jolt when I rode over curbs. It was a Cadillac of bikes, and the price tag at the bicycle shop said $60.

I saved my allowance—25 cents a week—and earned a little extra, and when I finally had $60 in hand I put the cash in a white envelope, printed my name on the outside in large block letters, and took the bus downtown. But somewhere between the bus stop and the bike shop I lost the envelope. Re-tracing my steps, I found nothing, and no longer willing take the honesty of my fellow man for granted, I went home disconsolate, knowing I'd have to put off my dream and start the long savings process all over again. That afternoon a man called to say he had found the envelope, the $60 still inside. Whether or not he recognized the writing as that of a small boy, the contents of the envelope as a small boy's dream, that good citizen—a person I never met—effectively forestalled my imminent tendency to doubt the universal goodness of my fellow man. I picked up my new bike that same day, quickly putting red, white, and blue streamers on the handle grips to heighten the appearance of speed.

◆   ◆   ◆

In the summer of 1950, when we were 11 and 12, Mom and Pop announced that Paul and I were going to Camp White Earth on White Earth Lake in Northern Minnesota. I suppose many boys would have been thrilled to go to summer camp, but I wasn't; summer camp couldn't possibly be better than my own backyard. My resistance to the idea was quick, intense, and irrelevant. We were going to camp, Mom and Pop said. We'd live in cabins, about 20 boys to a cabin, where we'd sleep in bunk beds; we'd use outdoor toilets and bathe in the lake and have campfires and learn to sail and we'd shoot at the rifle range. They explained all this with unconvincing enthusiasm. "They're just trying to get rid of us," Paul and I grumbled to each other.

I wasn't surprised that I loathed summer camp exactly as much as I thought I would. Even at age 11, I had an aversion to external discipline and regimen applied with heavy hands, so it wasn't a good omen when on the first morning a feverishly ringing bell woke us from our sleep, a signal to leap from our bunks, grab our towels and soap dishes, and run barefoot and naked down a stony path for a chilly plunge in the lake. It wasn't that I minded getting up early or even plunging into cold water to bathe, but—in an early sign that I'd never be suited to the military life—having to do all those things with others and on somebody else's command was odious to me.

Even though White Earth wasn't a military camp, some of the counselors seemed determined to make it one. The counselors in my cabin—Cal Stoll and Gordy Soltau, both Big Ten football players at the University of Minnesota—were sadists: If a camper didn't roll out of bed fast enough for Cal, Cal tipped the bed over on him, even if the boy were in the upper bunk. He walked shirtless around the cabin, a marksmanship medal pinned to his bare chest. Gordy used a canoe paddle to swat troublesome campers. There was absolutely no reason to doubt the rumor that if you irritated Gordy or Cal, they dragged you from your cabin at night, stripped you to your underwear, and tied you to a tree as mosquito bait. (Their early training as sadists paid off. Cal Stoll later became head football coach at the University of Minnesota and Gordy Soltau played tight end for the San Francisco 49ers.)

There was a rifle range where we earned medals for shooting, and there was a fleet of sailboats that we learned how to sail, but the preeminent activity at this camp was swimming. (One of the camp's owners, Neils Thorpe, was a university swim coach, and some campers wondered if this might be a summer training ground where he could lure candidates for his team.) A camper's progress in swimming, unlike his progress in other activities, was recorded on a large chart on the wall of the dining room, awards were presented for swimming achievement, and the strongest swimmers were held up as idols to the younger boys. There was even a camp swim team that traveled to meets in nearby towns, and the rest of us were shanghaied in chartered school buses to make up a cheering squad.

I'm not sure what impelled me—it was probably the thought of my name on that hallowed chart on the dining room wall, and maybe the lure of physical challenge—but I privately resolved that even though I'd never swum more than a few yards before, by the time the session was over I would swim half a mile. It would be another of those occasions when I'd assert myself not through words but through some kind of physical act.

On the late afternoon when I made my attempt, there was no one on the waterfront to interfere by reminding me that by swimming alone, I was breaking the rules. A long dock reached out into the lake and, to the left—50 yards from the dock—was a floating platform for diving. I'd have to make eight round trips to reach my goal.

I slipped into the water and began to swim, knowing that I'd just have to take it slowly and steadily, that even though I was no swimmer, I was strong enough and stubborn enough to do it. As I thrashed unseen through the water late that summer afternoon, my face pointed upward to keep water out of my eyes, I was a picture less of athletic grace than of plain old grit. But I don't think I ever doubted I'd finish; it was just a matter of persistence. And I persisted. Back and forth. Back and forth. Eight times. For much of the time the main obstacle was boredom; later it was fatigue. When I finally finished the 16th lap, my arms were rubbery and I was almost unable to wriggle out of the water on to the dock. As I'd neared the end I'd thought about going further, 200 yards maybe, but decided 800 yards was enough. I'd leave it at that.

That evening in the dining room I announced my accomplishment to Cal, eager to see my name inscribed on the chart.

"When did you do this?"

"This afternoon."

"There was no swimming period this afternoon."

"I know. I just went down to the swimming beach by myself."

His eyes narrowed and he glanced at the other counselors.

"Who were your witnesses? Who was spotting?"

He was sounding like Pop after I'd read *Two Years Before the Mast.*

"I didn't have any. I just did it. By myself."

He stood there looking at me, then at the other counselors, and they all glanced uneasily at each other while I silently berated myself for my naiveté.

They could doubt my word and insist on a witness, and since I didn't have one, and since I'd broken the rule about swimming alone, they could withhold an award and the recording of my name on the dining room chart, thereby ensuring an embittered young camper and the birth of a cynic. Or they could compromise their own reasonable standards, give me the benefit of the doubt, reluctantly acknowledge an unverified achievement, and try to salvage my sense of achievement.

Resolve had worked before when I wanted out of piano lessons, so I tried it again.

"I swam 800 yards," I said firmly, looking over at the chart.

The counselors mumbled and shuffled around for a few minutes, then eventually gave in and inscribed my name on the chart on the wall, but they made sure I knew they weren't happy doing it, that they didn't believe I'd done what I said I did. So even though they'd done the right thing, my achievement was less satisfying than it could have been because, like Pop, they'd doubted my word, and their undisguised skepticism left me indignant and sour. Adults ought to be better than this, I thought.

There were a few other agreeable activities at camp—crafts, for example. I spent time making key chains and other useless artifacts, but it was a quiet, solitary pastime and it kept me away from Gordy and Cal. Tennis was agreeable too—I learned to play the game there—and so were evening campfires—at that age I was still amused by songs like "Ninety-nine Bottles of Beer on the Wall."

On Sundays, though, for reasons I never knew and would probably have rejected if I did, we were required to dress all in white. I didn't know the words *ludicrous* or *foppish* then; but I knew what ludicrous and foppish *felt* like, and I didn't like it. There were also compulsory afternoon rest periods when we were to lie quietly in our bunks and write letters home. I compliantly got out my pencil and notepaper and painfully squeezed out a few sentences. Mom saved those letters from camp, and I hold one of them in my hands now. It's scrawled in pencil on Cub Scout stationery, originally white but now faded to ivory, and across the lower left corner, in blue ink, are printed a trail of bear tracks.

Dear Mom,

Can you guess what we had to eat today? We had something that tasted like boiled saw-dust and nobody liked it. One of the councilers Gordy Soltau has a handle of a canoe padle that he swats the noisy kids with. Swimming is lots of fun too.

My favorite camp activity was undoubtedly an illegal one, and had I been caught at it, the counselors would probably have stripped me to my underwear and fed me to the mosquitoes. Late one afternoon I went down to the beach where the canoes lay belly up on the grass. They were beautiful boats—Old Towne, wood, covered with dark green canvas. I rolled one over and enjoyed looking at the wooden ribbing, gunwales, seat frames, and thwarts—all beautifully varnished, all warm in the afternoon sun. I chose a stern paddle, dragged the canoe to the water's edge, and silently shoved off. Paddling along the shore to my right, I soon rounded a point and headed into a small, shallow bay. Lily pads ringed the edge of the bay, and beyond them cattails, then tall aspens and conifers that had begun to throw long shadows over the water. Protected from wind, the bay was quiet and I could hear the croaks of frogs, the trill of red wing blackbirds, and the faint rustle of aspen leaves from the shore. I just sat quietly in the stern of the canoe, the paddle resting across the gunwales, water dripping off the blade and making little tapping sounds on the glassy surface of the bay. In the cattails I found an old redwing blackbird nest with an abandoned egg in it. I removed the egg from the nest, placed it carefully in my shirt pocket, and brought it back to camp where I kept it safe in a small box. If camp were like this, I thought, maybe I could enjoy it.

Like that troubled little kindergarten boy who didn't know how to fit in, I was still uncomfortable among people whose company I didn't choose. But there was a difference now. Somehow in the six years since that terribly lonely year when all my neighborhood friends started school ahead of me, by age 11, I had learned to appreciate solitude, and given the choice of unsought and unwelcome companionship or being alone, I much preferred being alone.

In the four weeks Paul and I were at Camp White Earth in that summer of 1950, we were almost fully shielded against news from the outside world, but two events broke through. One afternoon as I was walked out of our cabin, someone told me we were at war in Korea, wherever *that* was. The other was the boxing match between "Jersey Joe" Walcott and Ezzard Charles for the heavyweight championship of the world. We weren't exposed to news of the war, but one night in the camp kitchen behind the dining hall, under a canopy of industrial-size pots and pans, spatulas and spoons, one counselor and a handful of boys sat around a long table covered in checkered oilcloth and listened to the fight on a small radio perched on a shelf above the sink. In the seventh round Walcott knocked out Charles and became the new, world heavyweight champ. Having never heard of Korea, I thought the boxing match more significant.

6

You are told a lot about your education, but
some beautiful, sacred memory, preserved
since childhood, is perhaps the best education
of all. If a man carries such memories into
life with him, he is saved for the rest of his days.

The Brothers Karamazov—

Feodor Dostoyevsky

In my memory, fall is the most glorious time of year. When the leaves begin to turn, the lush green of summer recedes and a deep yellow advances, the yellow of the fall elms arching over the streets. But fall never lasts long enough. Too soon the trees are bare, and after the freeze the ground is iron-hard and the sky is iron gray, and snow is welcome because it brightens the landscape again.

When winter arrived Pop delivered his annual recitation of The River Rule, one of the few household rules I remember. There were plenty of *other* rules everyone grew up with then: Shake hands when you're introduced, take your hat off indoors, excuse yourself when leaving the table, don't make a fool of yourself in public, be courteous to others. But The River Rule was unique to our house, and as soon as ice formed on the river each winter, Pop dragged out The River Rule, dusted it off, and delivered it once again from the pulpit of domestic authority: "Don't go on the ice until the temperature has twice dropped to twenty below."

So until we had two minus-twenties we had to find other things to do. The neighborhood gang dug caves into the high mounds of snow piled along the driveway and sidewalks; or with large clumps of snow we'd make forts for protection in neighborhood snowball fights. When we were a little older, ten or eleven, we hitched cars, waiting at intersections for cars to stop, pretending to be occupied with something else, then grasped the rear bumper with mittened hands and glided over the snow-packed street as the car picked up speed. It was a good ride if you went a block or two, a bad ride if you hit a patch of bare pavement or a layer of cinders laid down by the city to give vehicles traction at intersections.

Until there was enough snow for sliding on the hill, or until the river ice was safe, I hunted and trapped along the river south of town. When I was old enough to use a gun by myself—first my Daisy lever action BB gun, later a single shot, bolt action pellet gun powered by a CO2 cartridge—I began my Daniel Boone phase, trekking along the river, following the dirt road between the river and the golf course and looking for things to kill. When I had the BB gun, living things didn't have much to fear, but with a fully-charged pellet gun I could drop squirrels and small birds and cultivate the feeling that I was a genuine hunter. Later, when I was allowed to use one of Pop's .22's, I increased my killing power and felt more adult. His Marlin lever action was my favorite. I liked the feel and balance of it; and the hexagonal barrel gave it kind of an antique touch that better fit my Daniel Boone image.

My first kills were red and gray squirrels. After a successful hunt I headed home along the river, the Marlin lever action in one hand and a cluster of dead squirrels hanging by their tails from the other. I'd heard that squirrels could be turned into pies—another of Pop's rules was that you eat what you kill—but Mom refused to cook them, apparently having been infected by the prejudice that a squirrel is nothing but a rat with good public relations.

If I couldn't eat the squirrels, I thought, at least I could skin them, preserve the pelts, and line gloves with them, so I took them to the basement where I went at them with the Xacto knives I'd gotten for Christmas. I began with a long slit from chin to anus, then slit up the inside of each leg, slicing my fingers almost as much as I did the squirrels. Eventually I was able to rip the pelts from the body and tack them spread-eagle on a board to dry. But when I removed the pelts from the board they weren't soft and supple as I'd expected but disappointingly brittle, and I was discouraged even more when I discovered that in skinning squirrels, not only had I butchered my fingers, I'd become a host for lice. All in all there wasn't much to encourage me in squirrel hunting life.

When I was about 12, a new neighborhood friend named Bill McDonald convinced me to forget about squirrels and to go in for something more lucrative: trapping mink. Bill was a profane, hot-tempered kid with thick glasses and an enviable ability to spit great distances.

Mink coats are expensive, Bill told me; there's a lot of money to be made in the trapping end of the business. A whole career, he said. Bill was a year or two older and therefore knew what he was talking about, so I followed him downtown to Secord's sporting goods store where we bought some leg-hold traps and vials of foul smelling mink scent which we kept tightly capped. Bill even knew to thrust the traps in boiling water, then dip them in melted paraffin to rid them of human odors.

One day after school, we headed out along the river to set up our trap line, laying the traps near patches of open water, staking them down, and sprinkling the foul-smelling mink scent nearby. The way I figured it, we'd catch a bunch of mink, turn them into coats, and rake in the riches, all by the end of the week.

Every day after school, Bill and I took turns checking our trap line. Pulling on a wool stocking cap, warm gloves, a loose-fitting parka, and insulated boots, I grabbed the Marlin lever action and headed out along the river to the south. The winter sun sets early at 48 degrees north latitude, so there wasn't much time to check all the traps and get home before dark. Trudging out faithfully along the river, often through thigh-deep snow and the unforgiving North Dakota cold, I was propelled partly by the enjoyment of being outdoors alone in this harsh, austere world, partly by the twin forces of optimism and the lure of fabulous wealth.

It was a great puzzle to me on my first day to find nothing in the traps. It was an increasingly greater puzzle when they were empty the day after that, and the rest of the week, and the rest of the winter. We tried moving our traps to more promising sites; we tried more liberal sprinklings of scent; but nothing seemed to work, and it was getting more and more difficult to muster the optimism and energy it took for that solitary trudge through the snow and the cold.

One cold, iron gray afternoon in our second trapping season, I found a mink in one of the traps. At least I *assumed* it was a mink; I'd never seen one before. It was an elongated, low-slung, gray-brown mammal, pointy eared, a little larger than a weasel, and still very alive. He was caught by a hind leg and was darting frantically about, his range limited by the 12 inch chain that linked the trap to the stake.

Now that I finally trapped a mink I wasn't sure what to do with it. If he'd been dead, I'd simply have brought him home and used him as the centerpiece of a coat; but this mink wasn't dead, and although I wasn't sure what to do, I knew I'd have to kill it. I'd brought along the .22—that's just what trappers did—but even as a boy I knew no one would pay top dollar for a mink coat with a bullet hole in it, so I scrambled furiously through the snow, found a blunt stick, and tried to club him to death. The mink lunged frantically back and forth within his twelve-inch radius and evaded my blows. I swung many times but struck nothing but frozen ground. Then suddenly in one of his lunges the mink somehow slipped loose from the trap, darted for the patch of open water nearby, and slipped out of sight. As I stood there in the biting air listening to the thumping of my heart, I could think only of the fortune that had just vanished through that little hole in the ice and of the career that had disappeared with it.

When my breathing was finally calm again, I realized the sun had already set so I turned around and followed my tracks toward home, thinking as I plodded through the thigh-deep snow that after all these fruitless trips along the river to check the traps, after the collapse of this dream of great wealth, I at least had a story to tell, even if it was a disappointing one. It was dark by the time I got back to the house, and as I walked up the hill, the lights from the windows made warm, yellow rectangles on the snow.

After trapping, my next get-rich scheme was door-to-door sales of magazine subscriptions and Christmas cards. In retrospect, my failure in sales isn't surprising. I was stymied not just by my discomfort in meeting people but by the very *idea* of selling—the cunning process of convincing someone to buy something he hadn't asked for and probably didn't even need. So I never developed a sales pitch, never overcame the aversion to walking up somebody's front steps and ringing the bell, even a neighbor's, and I was derailed too by the suspicion that a purchase would be motivated more by a feeling of neighborly obligation than by genuine need. Having already shown signs that I lacked the temperament and talent for music, the tolerance for military discipline, and the skill for trapping, I could now list sales as one of the ways I'd never make a name for myself.

I had one other experience with the world of commerce at this point, and it involved Charles Atlas, another of my childhood idols. As one of those boys who wanted a good physique, I looked at Charles Atlas as an exemplary specimen. Anyone could see from the ad on the backs of comic books that he was ideally proportioned, evenly tanned and nicely muscled. I was seduced by that image and by the thought that within a few days I could convert my scrawniness into a Charles Atlas shape, streamlined and well muscled. I don't remember what product was being sold, but I sent in my money. I hadn't forgotten that I'd succumbed to other ads before—a magic decoder ring pitched on one of the Saturday morning radio shows, for example—and that I'd been disappointed; like a "prize" from a box of Cracker Jacks, it was nothing but a cheap trinket. But that was just something for kids. This was different.

While I waited, I entertained myself with visions of my body-to-be. It wouldn't be an overly developed, heavily greased body with those grotesque ropes of muscles you see in the body builders' magazines. My new body would have broad shoulders with smooth, nicely shaped muscles, especially in the upper arms and abdomen, a narrow waist, and nicely muscled but not bulging calves. Deeply tanned, it would be striking in a white swimsuit.

I had plenty of time to indulge in these fantasies, because weeks went by with nothing arriving in the mail, and then more weeks, and gradually my faith began to falter, and finally it vanished altogether. I'd been taken, I realized. I was stuck with the scrawny body I had, and the world of advertising gave birth to yet another skeptic.

◆   ◆   ◆

The hill in our backyard, the longest and steepest in town, was the best hill in town for sliding; so on a Saturday morning when the snow was deep enough to cover the grass, the neighborhood gang and even boys from other parts of town—some whom we'd never seen before—showed up at our house with sleds, skis, flying saucers, toboggans, even scraps of cardboard and cardboard boxes—anything they could ride to the bottom of the hill.

With a new sled, you first had to sandpaper the paint from the bottom of the runners. Then you took a running start, belly-flopping on the sled and racing downward, and when the snow was packed, you might go the hundred yards to the river, and if you got to the river, the extra momentum you picked up by going down the bank might get you clear to the Minnesota side.

To increase the danger, near the bottom of the steepest part of the hill we piled up snow to form a ramp about two feet wide and five feet long with a two foot drop at the end, then loaded a toboggan with as many boys as possible, usually about five, and took it over the ramp, thrilled to be airborne for a moment before hitting the snow with a loud *whump*. Sometimes a boy on a sled tried to pass *under* the toboggan while it was still in the air, a feat that usually failed when the toboggan crashed on top on him.

In another game we called Fighter Pilot, a fully loaded toboggan started down the hill, the boy in the rear—the tail gunner—facing backwards and holding fireplace logs in his lap. Other boys on sleds tried to catch the toboggan and pull somebody off. To defend against attacks, the tail gunner pitched logs in front of the sleds. What made the game fun was that no matter who won, the hill was littered with bodies.

I don't remember ever *not* sliding because of cold. Wrapped in our stocking caps, winter coats, chopper mittens and black, buckle overshoes, we went up and down that hill from morning 'til dark, making thirty to forty round trips a day on weekends. When we went inside for supper Saturday night, eventually our toes began to thaw and the thawing ached; but Sunday morning we were out again, going down and up, down and up, until the lights in the house went on and it was too dark outside to see.

One winter, Tommy Hoghaug's father showed us a world of new possibilities when he got out his garden hose and flooded his little backyard to make a skating rink, and from then on hockey was the only winter game in the neighborhood. What basketball is to Indiana or football to Texas, hockey is to North Dakota. Every year the University team was one of the best college teams in the country and the high school team one of the best in the Upper Midwest. As children we often went to the university and high school games, then came home and tried to emulate our heroes, at first on our snow-packed street, using real hockey sticks and a puck but wearing our black, buckle overshoes in place of skates and using a couple of chunks of snow to delineate the goal.

But when Dr. Hoghaug flooded his little backyard and made real ice, our hockey games took a major step upward. Most of us already had skates—hockey skates, of course; when a boy showed up one day in figure skates we laughed him off the ice—most of us already had sticks, and someone usually showed up with a puck. And that was the extent of our equipment. Only sissies wore helmets, shin guards, padded gloves or mouthpieces, so by season's end we had bruised knuckles and battered shins as proof of our toughness.

But one winter some neighborhood innovator improvised shin guards by taping magazines around his lower legs under his trousers. The idea caught on and soon all of us were taping magazines around our shins, *National Geographic* for us shorter boys, *Life* or *Saturday Evening Post* for the taller ones. They didn't protect the knees, of course, but they protected everything between the knees and the ankles, and that was a great step forward, a sign that we weren't entirely immune to common sense.

When we outgrew the Hoghaug rink, which wasn't much bigger than our living room, we moved on to our next, much large rink—the ice of the Red River. We armed ourselves with snow shovels one winter morning and cleared a sheet of ice the size of a real hockey rink. The river ice was never as smooth as we wanted it to be—if snow had been falling at freeze-up, the surface was sandpaper coarse; if we'd had wind, the surface was pebbly. And with the rink so far from the house, we couldn't run a garden hose down the hill to resurface it. But the size of the rink overcame those little drawbacks, and for two to three winters, river hockey was the hottest game in our end of town.

About the time these games moved to the river, we began wearing more sophisticated equipment—real hockey shin guards and real hockey gloves were acceptable now—but we drew the line at helmets; helmets, like figure skates and skinny-tired bikes, were for sissies.

Paul and I and the Grinnell brothers next door could put on our skates in the warmth of home, then just walk down the hill to the rink, but most boys hooked their skates over the blades of their sticks, walked from home to the rink, some from up to a mile away, and sat down in the snow at rink side to lace on their skates.

The first ones to arrive on Saturday would simply skate around on our own, practicing passing and stick handling, warming up, waiting. That was my favorite time on the rink; before other skaters arrived, you could enjoy the sound of your blades as you carved a turn, and as you slapped the puck with the blade of your stick you heard the sound again as it echoed off the riverbanks. When four or five more players arrived, we divided into teams and the game was on.

Since the rink was enclosed by snow banks rather than boards, there was no body checking in these games. We also banned "lifting" the puck, which would have meant losing too many pucks in the deep snow. We tried to balance the teams in strength, and we tried to observe the customary bans on tripping and high-sticking, but there were no referees and no penalty box, so these games on the river were wild, unregulated affairs that might have been mistaken for chaos.

By midday the players who'd arrived early might get hungry and leave for lunch, but by then others arrived so the teams kept changing as the day went on; a player might be on one team at the start of the day but switch sides several times before the game was over at dusk when the make-up of teams might have little resemblance to what it was in the morning. Still, the game flowed on seamlessly throughout the day, sometimes with as many as eight per side.

But as winter wore on, maintaining the rink became more burdensome. The job of shoveling always seemed to fall on those of us who lived along the river, and there was the ongoing problem of patching the cracks that formed with changes in temperature. They happened suddenly, often sounding like rifle shots echoing up and down the river, and even though the ice was two feet thick, it was always unnerving to hear that sound and see the crack appear suddenly beneath your skates. We tried hauling water down the hills in pails and forming a slush that we tamped into the cracks like spackle on drywall, but the frozen slush crumbled quickly, and soon we were catching our skates in the cracks again and breaking the blades.

After a couple of these hockey seasons on the river, the city Park Board established a real rink on Lincoln Park Golf Course just off Belmont Road. It had real boards and real goals at each end and was re-surfaced once a week. There was even a warming house staffed by a gray, grizzled guy who kept a fire going in an old barrel stove. With these kinds of luxuries we didn't mind walking half a mile across the golf course through the snow to get there, and if we got cold we could always go indoors to warm up and amuse ourselves by spitting on the old barrel stove and watching it sizzle. It was our version of the Good Life.

Many years later when I returned to Grand Forks as an adult with children of my own, I was sometimes confused by changes that had taken place in town. I drove in on an interstate highway that hadn't existed before. The downtown business district had died when stores moved to the mall. New roads led to old places and old roads led to new ones. Familiar landmarks were gone. There were shopping centers where potato fields had been, and more chain restaurants than I'd remembered before. The Rays' farm had become a golf course. I wasn't sure any more how to get from one place to another. I felt as if I were in somebody else's town.

But one cold winter morning I got up early and went for a jog, exploring some familiar streets where friends lived long ago in houses now filled with strangers. It was a Sunday, and I could run down the middle of the snow packed streets. My route took me past a city park where we used to skate as boys, and there I was heartened by a familiar sight—a group of small boys playing hockey on an out-door rink. The temperature was around zero, the wind chill minus fifteen or 20. With stocking caps pulled over their ears and scarves tied tightly over their noses and mouths, they seemed oblivious to the cold. Here, I told myself, finally, is something that hasn't changed. Here, finally, is an immutable fact of North Dakota life: a tolerance for discomfort, a combative spirit un-intimidated by the severity of winter, and a readiness to accept the worst of it. I felt I was home again.

◆　　◆　　◆

Sometimes on Saturday mornings before going out to skate or slide, we listened to our favorite half-hour serials on radio—"The Lone Ranger," "Sky King," and "Sgt. Preston of the Yukon"—those indefatigable defenders of law and upholders of justice who stood ready each week to ensure that criminals were caught, that evil was foiled and right prevailed. In the world of Saturday morning radio, we could be sure that no one would ever confound us with moral ambiguities.

We found this same certainty in evening programs like "The FBI in Peace and War" and "The Shadow." Imagine how reassuring it was to know that the FBI was steadfast and diligent in guarding us against the enemy, both foreign and domestic, and that Lamont Cranston as The Shadow, with his uncanny power to cloud men's minds, was able to apprehend criminals as no one else. "The weed of crime bears bitter fruit," the announcer reminded us each week. "*Crime does not pay.*"

On Sunday nights when we listened to "The Jack Benny Show," we heard Jack go down the long, stone staircase to the underground vault where he squirreled his cash, and the sound effects took us along with him. When he spoke with Ed, the longtime employee who guarded the vault, that slow-motion, subterranean figure whose voice was covered with cobwebs, we could visualize this man who hadn't seen his boss for months and hadn't seen daylight for years. We'd heard this same scene many times before, but each time there was a new twist and each time it was funny—to adults *and* children—with no laugh track to tell us so.

Several years later some of these same shows appeared on television, but they were never as entertaining as they'd been on radio. To the human voices and sound effects on radio, we had to add imagination ourselves, and the evocative experience that came of it all was something that television will never afford. Whatever television has added to our lives, it has done so insidiously and at some expense.

On Saturday afternoons the neighborhood gang would sometimes ride the bus downtown for a movie. If we were feeling pinched, we'd go to the Forx where for nine cents we could see old Marx Brothers movies or The Three Stooges and where the manager, a wiry, white-haired, pink-faced geezer with thick, black-rimmed glasses, would sometimes shut off the projector, turn on the lights, and come down the aisle to threaten us into silence with a long, wagging finger.

I preferred to go to the Paramount and pay four cents more for a western with Gene Autry or Roy Rogers, or a comedy with Abbott and Costello or Laurel and Hardy. Besides better movies, for those four extra pennies we also got Warner Brothers cartoons like Bugs Bunny, The Roadrunner, or Sylvester with Tweety Bird and Yosemite Sam, and besides the feature film there was usually a serial starring Zoro or the Black Whip, each episode ending in tantalizing suspense: "Will Zoro be crushed by the boulder tumbling down the mountain?" "Will the Black Whip escape from the pit of poisonous snakes? Come back next week!" And each week were the newsreels—"The Eyes and Ears of the World"—where I saw my first footage of the strutting, maniacal Hitler and his goose-stepping followers. Sometimes there was even a sing-along in which we could "follow the bouncing ball" as it guided us through the rhythms of well known songs like "Red River Valley" or "I've Been Working on the Railroad."

On other winter days we played indoors with Tinker Toys and Lincoln Logs, a precursor to Legos, and later we had a hand-me-down Erector Set that came from a relative, and Electric Football, a competitive game for two.

One year Mom and Pop gave us an electric train for Christmas, a Lionel "O" gauge that we set up on the carpet at one end of the living room where it stayed for much of the winter. We had no interest in creating a miniature world surrounding the railroad, no interest in building elaborate towns with electric lights in little houses and smoke coming out of chimneys. We were more attracted to power and speed, to a model railroad version of Demolition Derby. Using a set of wooden blocks, we built a barricade on the tracks, then threw the transformer to full throttle and sent the engine flying against the wall, the goal being to break through the barricade without derailing the engine.

◆   ◆   ◆

Part of my education in these pre-teenage years included an obligatory brush with religion, an enterprise that in retrospect was doomed to failure. I know that as a girl, Mom had gone to the Baptist church in Cavalier, but I don't know what Pop's religious background was. When she and Pop were married they attended the Presbyterian Church in Grand Forks, and that's where I dabbled inauspiciously in church and religion.

In our elementary school years when Paul and I began going to Sunday school in the church basement, the minister was Reverend Abernathy, a native Scot with an almost unintelligible brogue. When he addressed the boys and girls of the Sunday school, *girls* sounded like *gulls*, and in the effort it took to decipher his dialect I often forgot what he'd said.

But we had much less to do with Reverend Abernathy than we did with Mrs. Sutton, the head of the Sunday school who led us in our religious activities, one of which was "Jesus Loves Me."

It didn't take long for me to develop an intense dislike for this song—for the words, for the melody, for the whiney sound of my little co-religionists singing it—and sometimes I think maybe "Jesus Loves Me" was to blame for getting me off on the wrong foot with religion. But Mrs. Sutton may have had a part in it too; she was too syrupy for my taste and too fond of "Jesus Loves Me." But it wasn't just Mrs. Sutton and "Jesus Loves Me." Jesus himself put me off. Several pictures of him looked down on us from the Sunday school wall, one a portrait showing shoulder-length hair and his gentle mouth and eyes, another a full-length rendition in which he wore a white, ankle-length robe and sandals on otherwise-bare feet. I just didn't like his looks. I tried to make allowances for the fact that he lived a long time ago when clothing styles and hairstyles were different, but I couldn't shake the feeling that he looked like a sissy. By this point in my life my idols were Joe DiMaggio, Jackie Robinson, Doak Walker, and Johnny Lujack, so this soft-looking, sandal-shod guy in the pictures just didn't measure up, and his "Suffer-little-children-to-come-unto-me" approach didn't do the trick either.

All of these trappings of Presbyterian Sunday school made me uneasy, but to tell the whole story, I was uncomfortable before I ever left the house, dressed as I was in a white shirt with a starchy collar, an itchy red sweater with a large black bear woven into the front, and heavy corduroys that *whooshed* when I walked. Between my Sunday school clothes and the ministry of Mrs. Sutton, I felt doubly punished.

But on June 13, 1948, at age nine, I completed this first phase of my religious training simply by having taken up space in class, and on that occasion I was presented a *King James Bible* inscribed with that date and signed by Mrs. Sutton. Presumably, armed with this book, I was ready for confirmation classes, the next untoward phase of my religious instruction.

◆   ◆   ◆

Spring was the most awkward season for playing outdoors. Once the snow started to melt and the grass began peeking through, sliding was over for the season, and when the river ice softened and turned to honeycomb, hockey was finished too. As long as we still had patches of snow, the ground was too mushy for baseball or other summertime games. Fortunately, this awkward, sloppy-wet season was shorter than all the others.

The main event in those dull spring weeks was the occasional Red River flood. As early as January or February, adults began discussing the flood prospects for April and May. Meteorologists reported on snow depths up river at Fargo and speculated on the rate of snow melt, but flood forecasting was less sophisticated then, so life in spring was marked with greater uncertainty; farmers fretted about getting into the fields to plant, and residents along Lincoln Drive began worrying again about being driven out of their homes.

When the river finally did begin rising upstream we'd start getting daily reports from Fargo. The river is at 22 feet now. Now 27. Now 31. And eventually we knew when we went to bed at night that on the following morning the river would be out of its banks and rising toward our house and all the other houses along Lincoln Dive.

It was a dramatic sight when the river began to swell, even though it looked harmless at first. But then the ice broke and massive floes started moving downstream, and as the river spread, even with the current as slow as it is those large masses of ice toppled giant cottonwoods along the banks, and those floating cottonwoods in turn caused more damage of their own as they moved downstream.

Once the flooding began upstream at Fargo, our neighbors along the river listened anxiously for the flood forecasts and hung on the daily reports as the crest moved closer and closer to town, and from their experience they could pinpoint the day when they'd have to evacuate their homes. For some, the escape was a form of brinkmanship, and some of those made the move too late. Sometimes the National Guard was called into action for last-minute rescues with amphibious vehicles, and Red Cross workers waited at the edge of the water with warm blankets, hot coffee, and offers of clothing and shelter.

When the river swelled enough to drive people out of their homes, some of my Lincoln School classmates became refugees. I never thought to ask where they went when their homes were under water, what they had lost, if they needed clothes, how they felt about their plight. Since they continued with school, I guess I just assumed they were staying with friends or relatives nearby and that when the river subsided and their homes dried out, their parents would shovel the mud from their basements and living rooms and they'd move back in. I was too secure, too complacent to know about privation, too young to know about the molds that grew in homes after floods and about the dangers of contaminated water.

I just felt safely above all that in our home on the edge of the hill above the river in one of the highest parts of town. To me then, a flood wasn't so much a danger or a source of destruction as it was an adventure and an excitement. One morning I'd look out the window to see a normal river below me, and a few days later we'd have a lake in our backyard, a broad lake with large cottonwood trees growing in it, a lake that stretched far over the cornfields on the Minnesota side. For our amusement, my neighborhood friends and I would stomp on mice that—like the people on lower Lincoln Drive—were retreating to dry ground, or we'd hop onto ice floes and pole ourselves around the yard.

If the water rose high enough, there was the chance that it could pour into our house through a basement-level door on the river side and Pop would sandbag the entrance. Once in my childhood the river *did* reach that height, and the sight of all that water was overwhelming. Some water seeped through the sandbags, and in spite of the pump that Mom and Pop ran non-stop through the night, we had an inch or two of water in the basement. But nothing more.

It was when the river receded that the work began. After a couple of weeks of high water, the river left two to three inches of mud in the lower part of our yard, topsoil from farmers' fields upstream. As it baked in the spring sun and finally dried, it cracked and broke into chunks we could easily pick up, toss into a garden cart, and dump back into the river. In another month, we'd have a lush, green lawn again.

◆   ◆   ◆

In 1948, the same year the Presbyterians gave me the *Bible*, Mom and Pop gave me a Christmas present that interested me much more—Roger Tory Peterson's *Field Guide to the Eastern Birds*—and since then I have never been without a copy of it. I don't remember which came first—the book or my interest in birds; but before long I had memorized all 28 bird silhouettes that appear inside the front cover, and by the following spring I was keeping a life list, checking off birds in the back of the book and delighting each time my list expanded by one.

From our living room window and in my comings and goings around the neighborhood, I began to notice numerous birds to add to the list, but later, to see new species I had to go further afield, to take solitary excursions along the river or through the fields outside of town, and to go on family bird hunting trips in the fall when I added numerous waterfowl and upland birds. Even though I enjoyed playing with friends, with Peterson in my pocket I enjoyed trekking along the river alone or wandering the fields outside of town, scanning the tree-tops and the prairies for additions to my list.

As an offshoot to my collection of bird sightings, I later began a collection of bird eggs, starting with that redwing blackbird egg I'd found at Camp White Earth. One of the books in my parents' library was *Birds of America*, a heavy, 829-page volume with numerous color plates, including five color plates of bird eggs shown in actual size, ranging from the wren and the hummingbird to the Great Auk. I was fascinated by these plates and enjoyed simply looking at them, at the variations in size of the eggs and the slight variations in shape, at the sub-tlety of the colors and color patterns.

So I became a skilled climber of trees, sometimes going to dangerous heights to extract an egg, sometimes having to grasp a tree limb with one hand and wave off an angry parent bird with the other, sometimes climbing through numerous, close-set layers of spruce branches to extract a small white mourning dove egg, place it in my shirt pocket, and return to the ground with my hands covered with pitch, my arms scraped and bloody, and spruce needles in my hair, my ears, and my underwear.

To preserve and display these fragile little prizes, I chose a shirt box and lined it with cotton, then carefully placed the eggs in neat rows with small identifying labels that I had laboriously pecked out on Mom's typewriter. Eventually I expanded my collection to about two dozen eggs and kept it on my desk in my room. I prized all these eggs, some for their color or shape, some for the effort it had taken me to find it, some for their rarity.

My egg collection came to an end one day when the cleaning lady accidentally knocked the box to the floor and broke almost every one of them. The box of broken eggs stayed on my desk for months because I couldn't bring myself to throw them away, but eventually they went into the garbage and I looked for other things to collect.

Mom suggested stamps so I got a stamp book and pasted a few stamps in it, but I couldn't figure out the appeal of a stamp collection any more than I could figure out the appeal of religion so the stamp collection fizzled. Next I tried matchbooks. As friends of my parents learned about my collection they began picking up matchbooks for me and gradually I developed a respectable collection from far-flung places; but like most childhood hobbies, that one faded too, probably about the time I started to notice Judy Loft and Karen Ray, the only girls in our neighborhood. I wish I knew what became of all those matchbooks. Like an old photograph, like one of my letters from camp, like a bird egg, each has the power to revive a moment in a now-dead time, a far-away place.

◆   ◆   ◆

I also wish I could recall the chain of events that led me into the lilac bushes with Judy Loft. Judy would probably claim as historical fact that she had lived across the street from me all my life, but I would have bet my bird egg collection that she never popped into existence until I was about 11 or 12, and then mysteriously. I do remember this: that I began to notice her in the sixth grade at Lincoln and that she stood out because of her boldness and her lusty laugh. When our sixth grade chorus was rehearsing "Stout-hearted Men"—imagine a chorus of pre-adolescent voices pleading in song for stout-hearted men who will fight for the right they adore—Judy liked to throw out her burgeoning chest and shout, "Give me some men!" then laugh that lusty laugh. Maybe I took it as an invitation.

One warm summer evening between elementary school and junior high, Judy and I found ourselves together under the lilac bushes in front of the Ray's white, stucco house across the street from ours. I wish I could remember what brought us there, what we had been doing 10 minutes earlier, what signals we might have given each other that resulted in our convergence under the bush. I don't. But there we were. It was about 9:00 in the evening; dusk had just passed into darkness, and soon we'd have to go home. As we sat there under the lilac bush, leaning against the concrete foundation of the Ray's house, it was as if we were simultaneously struck by a realization that we had an opportunity here, an opportunity that might not soon come again. We were side by side, not even touching, not even holding hands. Then almost before I knew we were doing it, we were pecking each other quickly and repeatedly on the lips. Judy giggled nervously, and from her front door 50 yards away her mother's voice came through the darkness, "Judy, it's time to come in." Our time was running out. We stayed there just a little longer though, not talking, just squeezing in a few more quick pecks between giggles. Her mother called a few more times, then we scrambled out of the bushes and went our separate ways.

Judy and I met at least one more time under the lilac bush that summer, with equally pleasurable results, and on another occasion I found myself in the same location with her best friend Karen Ray, David's younger sister, a pretty, quiet girl with unusually large brown eyes and an alluring, bashful smile. By the end of the summer I could therefore truthfully claim that I had kissed every girl in the neighborhood, and on the basis of these field tests could pronounce that kissing girls was highly agreeable.

Discovering the pleasures of kissing is another one of those lurches or leaps in the haphazard, irreversible process of growing up, and once I'd made that discovery, I was never the same again. It didn't quite make me an adult, of course, but with hormones asizzle, with a newly expanded sense of life's possibilities, I was certainly far from the child I'd been just moments before.

7

To have come of age in the Forties was
to have one's maturity marked indelibly
by World War II. But to have come of
age in the Fifties was to miss being
swamped by public events, and, when you
come right down to it, to be a little out of
it was not a bad place to be.

"An Older Dude"—
Joseph Epstein

When I started junior high school in the fall of 1951, I was oblivious to most major events in the world, preoccupied as I was with grooming my new duck tail haircut, coping with pimples, trying to conceal my braces, and doing my damnedest to be cool. So I missed the lesser events of the time, like the founding of Israel, the Berlin airlift, the communist take-over of Czechoslovakia, the assassination of Gandhi and the collapse of the British Empire.

Yet I couldn't have been *completely* out of it because two events still stick like a burr to my memory. The first was announced loudly in the Grand Forks *Herald* earlier that year: "Truman Fires McArthur." We were Republicans in our family and had voted for Dewey in 1948. So how, I wondered in amazement, could that bespectacled runt from Missouri be so stupid as to fire the greatest general who ever lived? It serves Truman right, I thought, when McArthur was given a ticker tape parade in New York City and a hero's ovation in Congress. I sang along lustily as the popular song was played again and again on the radio, "Old soldiers never die; they just fade away." And I scoffed at Truman's prediction that the furor would die and that the rest of us too would one day recognize "Mr. Prima Donna, Brass Hat" for the "play actor and bunco man" he was, whatever *that* meant.

The other news stories that caught my attention all had to do with cheating, an uncommon occurrence in my small, moral, highly ordered world on the Northern Plains: the West Point cheating scandal in which 90 cadets were expelled; the television quiz show scandal in which contestants admitted having been fed answers to questions in producers' efforts to boost the ratings; and then the "payola" scandal in which radio disc jockeys were paid by recording companies to play certain songs again and again to give the illusion of popularity and boost record sales

My advancement to South Junior High School re-enforced my growing suspicion that the world wasn't quite as moral as I'd thought, as I wanted it to be. Because the junior high drew from a much wider radius, I came face to face with a larger slice of town—a boy whose older brother had been killed in a stolen car while being chased by the police, for example, and a girl who smoked and swore and who invited us to her house after school for smoking parties, a girl who satisfied my desire to dabble in what then passed for wickedness.

Distracted by such business, I have few memories of the academic part of those junior high years. The typing teacher, Miss Heller, a tall, sharp-edged woman with thick glasses, a perpetual frown, and thin, black hair with a bald spot on the crown, was one of those people who gave no sign that she found enjoyment in her work. "I-T space, I-T space," she repeated in a grim, machine gun style as she beat time on her wooden desk with a bony finger. In eighth grade, we studied something called "business math" in which we learned that interest equals principal times rate times time, or $I = PRT$, a fact of questionable value, it seemed to me. And in the ninth grade we got to start algebra, which finally seemed like real mathematics and which held my interest for exactly three more years.

In English we learned to identify parts of speech and the parts of a sentence, and eventually we began diagramming sentences, which was fun partly because it was easy, partly because—like the mechanical drawing we did in shop class and the geometry we learned later in high school—it appealed to my preference for order. At the time, never dreaming that some day I'd become an English teacher and a writer, I didn't see the value in it, any more than I saw the value of $I=PRT$. Mainly it was just another activity I was good at and that filled my adolescent need to feel superior to my classmates.

The one piece of literature I remember was Whittier's "Snowbound," which the teacher read aloud to us and which has stayed in my head for almost 50 years, maybe because to a North Dakotan it's so loaded with familiar images, like its ominous opening lines:

> *The sun that brief December day*
> *Rose cheerless over hills of gray,*
> *And, darkly circled, gave at noon*
> *A sadder light than waning moon.*

Slow tracing down the thickening sky
Its mute and ominous prophecy,
A portent seeming less than threat,
It sank from sight before it set.

I doubt that our teacher read us the entire 800 lines; when I read the poem today I find large sections that seem completely new to me—the long middle part, for example, where the snowbound captives in the farmhouse tell stories around the fire. But others bear the pleasing aroma of familiarity: the preparations for the imminent blizzard, the raging storm itself, and, when the storm was over, of the fantastic snow-covered world outside:

The old familiar sights of ours
Took marvelous shapes; strange domes and towers
Rose up where sty or corncrib stood,
Or garden wall, or belt of wood;
A smooth white mound the brush-pile showed.
A fenceless drift what once was road;
The bridle post an old man sat
With loose-flung coat and high cocked hat;
The well-curb had a Chinese roof;
And even the long sweep, high aloof,
In its slant splendor, seemed to tell
Of Pisa's leaning miracle.

That anyone could not only capture such familiar sights through words but do it in *rhyme* amazed me almost as much as the milkman's horse. At that age I certainly had no interest in performing such feats, but if I'd known that in 1866 Whittier pocketed $10,000 for the poem and that he'd left an estate worth $134,000, I might have been moved to take a crack at poetry myself, which would have been more lucrative than selling magazine subscriptions or trapping mink. Still, Whittier aroused my interest in literature, even though that interest wouldn't surface again until my second year at the University.

In my three years at South, the classes of least value to me were shop and physical education; no other classes matched them in uselessness. The shop teacher was a hard-nosed guy with a drill sergeant mentality and a wooden paddle. While he was concentrating his paddle on a boy who had maliciously gouged a table top with a wood plane, another boy behind him was busily gluing shut a woodworking vise. Those boys certainly got what they deserved, I thought, but at the same time the teacher was too reminiscent of the counselors at Camp White Earth.

While the girls in home economics were learning how to make pancakes, we boys in shop class were assembling small electric motors from kits. "Your motor will never work if you don't wind the copper wire carefully around the armature," the teacher warned us. "Each coil of the wire must lay neatly and closely to the preceding one. Take your time and your motor will work." The table-gougers and the vise-gluers laughed through this task with careless indifference, crisscrossing the wires and ending up with something that looked like a fishing reel with a backlash. I, on the other hand—a conscientious student with a preference for order—meticulously coiled the wire so that each wrap was neatly in place. The task took me much longer, of course, but what I ended up with was a far more aesthetic motor—neat, symmetrical, just like the one in the diagram. The troubling outcome was that mine didn't work while the others' did, and that presented problems for both the teacher and me. His problem was that contrary to what he wanted to teach, there was strong, incontrovertible evidence that slapdash works and following directions doesn't. Mine was the growing suspicion that adults were fallible, that when held up to the increasingly critical eye of the adolescent, they were sometimes found wanting, that Cal Stoll and Gordy Soltau were not aberrations.

Our physical education teacher Mr. Nelson—the same man who had supervised our games of Pursuit Race at Roosevelt and who'd been drafted during the war only to be rejected and turn up again at South—was a slender man who parted his short brown hair in the middle and had a soft-spoken manner that disguised his firmness. He insisted that we dress for class in clean shorts, tee shirts and tennis shoes and that we shower before going to our next class. The shower, I learned, is yet another device for separating the haves from the have-nots. Those who'd begun cultivating nice little crops of pubic hair were comfortable there, but those who hadn't usually showered with their backs to us, facing the wall.

If there was any benefit to me in those physical education classes, it came the morning I threw up on the gym floor in the midst of push-ups and, my arms still fully extended, studied the remains of my oatmeal breakfast splattered widely beneath me. The night before, two friends and I had stolen a beer from our refrigerator and split it three ways. Such was the sophistication of my reasoning that I saw a clear link between the one-third can of beer and the smell of vomit, so while some of my classmates took up beer drinking, the association of beer with vomit kept me abstemious throughout those years when I was striving for fame and glory in sports.

And for me, sports were the prime attraction at South Junior High; nothing else came close, not even girls. Unhindered by an interest in the academic side of my education, propelled by my earlier successes at Lincoln, lured by the camaraderie to which team sports are so conducive, I pledged eternal, unswerving loyalty to the fraternity of Jocks and began to see sports as the reason for my existence.

In junior high football we graduated from touch to tackle and finally got to wear real shoulder pads, rib pads, helmets, and real football shoes with real cleats. Coach Nelson also insisted that we wear athletic supporters with cups—"to protect your future family," he liked to say with a sly grin—and to illustrate what we should look for at the sporting goods store, he held up a sample supporter and cup and demonstrated how the cup slipped neatly into the pouch. Wearing the cup was uncomfortable, but if this was the price for playing in the big time, I was willing to pay it.

In our ninth grade year my football teammates and I were almost unstoppable. Today as I poke through the scrapbook in which I'd begun to memorialize my athletic diversions, I find—among yellowing newspaper clippings and the smell of mustiness—a scrap of paper on which I had written our record for the season: four wins and no losses. We outscored our opponents 93 to 7.

Winning football games in those chilly fall afternoons was great fun, of course, but no more fun than the bus rides home when—cold, sweaty, dirty, and tired,—we began singing songs soon after boarding the old orange bus and continued all the way back to the school. One of our favorites was "Stranger in Paradise" from the 1953 Broadway musical *Kismet*, a song of ardent love sung in duet.

> *Take my hand,*
> *I'm a stranger in paradise,*
> *All lost in a wonderland,*
> *A stranger in paradise.*

It was usually Kendall Cook who began the singing. A handsome boy with brown, wavy hair, clear skin, and a beautiful voice, he was enviably bold about soaring off into melodic heights. The rest of us quickly followed his lead.

> *If I stand starry-eyed,*
> *That's a danger in paradise*

For mortals who stand beside
An angel like you.

It didn't matter that some of our voices had changed and others' had not. Drunk with victory on the field, we had volume if nothing else, and our chorus rose above even the roar of the bus engine and the occasional grinding gears.

Won't you answer the fervent prayer
Of a stranger in paradise?
Don't send me in dark despair
From all that I hunger for.

We sang all the way into the locker room where we peeled off our sweaty uniforms and padding, and we continued into the steamy warmth of the shower where, with our voices ringing off the tile walls, we sounded even better.

But open your angel's eyes
To the Stranger in Paradise
And tell him that he need be
A stranger no more.

What the hell kind of outfit *is* this, Coach Nelson must have wondered. A team that clobbers its opponents and then sings *love* songs? We *were* an oddity, I suppose, a singing football team completely unconcerned about diluting our fervently cultivated image of male athleticism with songs of romantic love; and I'm wondering what to make of the fact that that singing is clearer and more indelible now than our record of wins and losses, which—unlike the lyrics to the song—I had to look up.

We were good at basketball too—the notes in my scrapbook show that we won 12 and lost just one. Our one loss was to the senior high school team in Manvel, a nearby farming community of 302 people where, on a Friday night in winter, the high school basketball game is the only show around. The whole town turned up and packed the cracker box gym where the walls were just a few feet beyond the boundaries of the court and the noise was intense and almost nonstop. We pulled into Manvel clothed in our big-city superiority, sniggering at the hickish appearance of the fans in their bib overalls and at the ugly, black-and-orange uniforms of the team and the cheerleaders. "This is beneath us," we thought, "playing these village clods who've just climbed off the tractor, even if they are in high school." It wasn't; they beat us 36 to 27. But then, as we told ourselves over and over on the ride back, "What the hell, 14-15 year olds aren't *supposed* to beat high school teams." Actually, we decided by the time we got home, we'd done pretty well to lose by only nine.

◆   ◆   ◆

But it was in track where I'd started to create the persona I'd wear for the rest of my school years, and my achievements in that sport in my last year of junior high school, much more so than our victories in football and basketball, were enough to seduce me with dreams of glory: In the city meet that year I took five first places and later at the spring awards assembly was called repeatedly to the stage to receive my blue ribbons. The pride and satisfaction of winning were mixed with the old discomfort of public attention and with the awkward, adolescent uncertainty about how to acknowledge compliments—it would have been far easier to have received those ribbons in the mail—but I damned well didn't object to a mention of my achievements in the mimeographed school newspaper. In the arduous business of building a persona, that kind of publicity only advances the cause, and since I was reluctant to be my own press agent, I welcomed all efforts of anyone willing to do the job for me.

That spring I was invited to join the high school track team while also competing on the team at South, so after school I took the city bus downtown to train with high school boys, some of whom shaved every day and had hair on their chests and were therefore indistinguishable from grown men, and at that point junior high sports suddenly became kid stuff.

Being on the high school track team meant wearing real track shoes with spikes instead of black tennis shoes, and real track uniforms—maroon with a silver slash across the chest. It meant using the *varsity* locker room at the high school, a dreary, cramped, odoriferous, subterranean cavern accessible only by a narrow, spiral stairway. (It had developed a dubious prestige simply because it could be used by varsity teams exclusively.) It meant competing in invitational meets with as many as 50 other schools. And it meant meets every weekend during the spring, including some at the University track; out-of-town meets as far away as Devil's Lake, Fargo, and Moorhead, some of which were overnight trips with stays in hotels. And it meant the prospect of qualifying for the state meet, held every year at Valley City. For a 15 year old who had chosen for himself the identity of Runner—someone whose heroes were no longer Charles Atlas and Daniel Boone, Robin Hood and the Black Whip but real life athletes like Roger

Bannister, who was close to breaking the four-minute mile, and Bob Mathias, who had won his first Olympic Decathlon in 1948 while still in high school and who had just won his second in 1952—all this was mighty hot stuff.

Coach Louie King (behind his back we called him King Louie) assigned me to what most people thought was the most loathsome running event in all of track, the 440 yard dash—in 1954, we were years away from metric distances—maybe less because he thought I was cut out for it than because he figured that as a ninth grader I wasn't bold enough to say "No." Whatever the case, as a docile junior high kid who felt honored just to be on the senior high team, I went along.

It took me much of a season to learn that event, but I placed in three meets that spring, and nothing puffed up my ego in that first year of high school track like qualifying for the state meet. No one expected me to place there, of course, and I didn't; at that age, just being there was enough. Running against the best in the state before a stadium filled with cheering spectators, reading my name in the glossy souvenir program, seeing the size of the medals awarded to the top three finishers—with all of that, it was hard to be disappointed in my sixth-place finish, especially knowing that in the following year I could possibly finish in the top three.

We try out various guises as we bumble through those teenage years, looking for one that fits; then, thinking we know who we are, we play that role with cautious uncertainty. At 15, I knew who I was. I was a runner. That would be my identity, I decided, my role in life, and full of myself as I was, I would play it to the hilt. I might try out a few other roles, but they'd be minor ones. I knew I was a runner, and I was already looking forward to the spring of my sophomore year and all the fame and glory ahead of me. Everything between now and then was inconsequential.

◆   ◆   ◆

The continuation of my religious studies also helped with this business of identity, if only because it showed who I was *not*. Just before beginning junior high, I made regular after-school jaunts to confirmation classes at the Presbyterian church where the new minister, Reverend Harry Sweitzer, a tall, thin, stern, balding man with dark hair, thick glasses, and long bony fingers, tried to clear away the mysteries surrounding religion and religious faith so that, inspired by the wisdom of God and the Lord Jesus Christ, I might become a person of moral worth and achieve full membership in the church.

Most of what I remember about confirmation classes was memorizing the Ten Commandments, the Beatitudes, and the names of the books of the *Bible*, all of which was easy enough because it required neither thinking nor understanding. But where I ran into trouble was with the idea of the Trinity. The Father and Son stuff seemed clear enough, but the Holy Ghost figure was amorphous and incomprehensible, and in spite of Reverend Sweitzer's patient efforts to explain it, I never could make sense of it.

The more fundamental barrier to my religious advancement was my inability to make the leap of faith. When I was younger I'd had a sort of tentative faith in the hoolihookoos, those ominous, legendary creatures that kept us away from the river; but at age six or seven that faith had been shaken, and apparently I was moving toward more critical thought, wondering how you can have faith in something you can't see or understand. Besides, having become a concrete thinker befuddled by notions like Holy Ghosts, it seems I was becoming a rationalist and an empiricist, if not an outright skeptic. To put it another way, I was becoming my father.

I kept these shortcomings to myself though, figuring they might block my membership in the church, which would be a failure and therefore unacceptable; so I have in my possession today—along with the grade school art work, my letters from camp, and all my report cards from grades one through 12—a certificate of church membership dated May 27, 1951, and signed by Reverend Sweitzer himself. As I look at this little document today, having not laid eyes on it in 49 years, I'm surprised by what I read:

> *I confess my faith in God the Father Almighty, Maker of heaven and earth, and in Jesus Christ, His only Son our Lord, and promise with the aid of the Holy Spirit to be Christ's faithful disciple to my life's end.*

> *I hereby confirm the vows taken for me in Baptism and with a humble and contrite heart put my whole trust in the mercy of God, which is in Christ Jesus our Lord.*

> *I promise to make diligent use of the means of grace, to share faithfully in the worship and service of the Church, to give of my substance as the Lord may prosper me, and to give my whole heart to the service of Christ and His kingdom throughout the world.*

"*Jesus Christ!*" I ask in amazement, "I promised *that?*" Evidently I was not only a rationalist and an empiricist but a humbug too. Instead of standing up and saying, "Hold on there; I'm not so sure I can go along with all that," instead of stirring up the proceedings with troublesome matters like conscience or intellectual integrity, I meekly went along with the routine.

Mom and Pop continued to insist that we go to church occasionally as a family, and not just on Christmas and Easter; Pop was an Elder in the church for a while, and I even sang in the church choir voluntarily while I was in high school. But Paul and I grumbled about having to dress up in jackets and ties on Sunday mornings and submit to the religious ritual, and eventually they gave up the battle: By the time we were in college the option of church attendance was left to us, which meant that we stopped going to church altogether. I was moving closer to the view of Ambrose Bierce, patron saint of cynics, that religion is "a daughter of Hope and Fear, explaining to Ignorance the nature of the Unknowable."

In retrospect, none of this is surprising. Our family was a thoroughly secular outfit. Mom and Pop never showed evidence of spirituality themselves; there were never discussions of religious matters around the dinner table, no praying or saying grace, never a mention of Jesus or God or Holy Ghosts. By sending us to Sunday school and confirmation classes and hauling us along to Sunday services, it seems they were adhering to what they saw as a parental duty, a duty I can hardly argue with, even though as a parent I never fulfilled it myself. All in all, it was an illustration of the futility of instruction un-buttressed by conviction.

They exposed us to travel too, but probably with greater belief in its benefits. For an immersion in glamour and excitement, they took us several times in my junior high years to Minneapolis and St. Paul, "the cities," where at Dayton's department store I took my first ride on an escalator and where we took the elevator clear to the top of the Foshay Tower, the tallest building in Minneapolis—at 440 feet, much taller even than the State Mill and Elevator in Grand Forks. From the observation deck we could see all the way to Elk River 30 miles away. We went to some Minneapolis Lakers games and watched the great George Mikan, "Mr. Basketball." As we strolled the city, we even saw a few Negroes, figures of great curiosity to a Dakota boy at mid century, and I tried hard not to stare.

One summer we took a trip to Chicago where my Aunt Doris and her husband Joe showed us Lake Michigan, the former home of Al Capone, and eccentric houses by someone named Frank Lloyd Wright. At the Museum of Science and Industry we descended by elevator into a coalmine, and at Comiskey Park where we watched the White Sox play the Yankees and the great Mickey Mantle, I saw even more Negroes than I'd seen in Minneapolis. It made me uneasy to be among so many people who were so different from me, and I puzzled over the fact that the backs of their hands were so dark while their palms looked just like mine. My Chicago cousins introduced us to *Mad* magazine and to The Carpenters, neither of which had yet reached the backwater of North Dakota, and at that point I began to wonder about all the *other* things I didn't know, to ask myself how many *other* developments had yet to reach Grand Forks, and I had my first sensation of being a small town hick just one short step above those people from Manvel.

On another trip to Chicago we went through Milwaukee where we saw a Braves game—the Braves hadn't yet moved to Atlanta—rode a ferry across Lake Michigan (the largest body of water I had ever seen), and stopped in Dearborn, Michigan, where on a tour of a Ford assembly plant I witnessed assembly-line manufacturing, an experience that watered the seed of cynicism: When a car rolled off the line and a worker discovered that the trunk wouldn't close, he clubbed at the latch with a rubber mallet until the lid stayed shut, then sent the car on its way to an unsuspecting buyer.

It was on one of these trips, a trip to Minneapolis, where I witnessed something that raised troublesome questions and has puzzled me ever since. Mom and Pop, Paul, Don and I were having lunch in one of the expensive restaurants, a restaurant with white linen tablecloths and waiters in black jackets and black ties. Pop was sitting directly across the table from me. After we'd ordered, a man—another customer—rose from his table and walked toward the door, passing directly behind Pop's chair where he suddenly collapsed on the floor. There was great commotion in the restaurant, of course, as waiters busied about the unconscious man, fanning him with white linen napkins and calling, "Is there a doctor in the house?" The man may have been dying; I don't know. What I do know is that my father, a doctor, needing only to turn around to give aid to the man on the floor, did nothing. Except for a nervous drumming of his fingers on the white linen tablecloth, he sat there as if he were oblivious to the distress right behind him, as if nothing were happening.

As I sat there in bewilderment, he avoided our eyes. A calculating, deliberate man, he always had some reason for his actions, but for what reason could he possibly withhold the assistance that his years of training and experience enabled him—obligated him—to give? He'll explain himself later, I thought, when we're in private. But he never did. Nor did I ask; I'd learned not to, having raised important questions before and gotten anger or impatience in return. Again an adult found wanting—this time my own father. Again an unanswered question. With each unanswered question, the chasm between us grew, and so did the likelihood that it would ever be overcome.

One summer when Paul and I were in junior high school and Don was about six, our family headed west through South Dakota (Wall Drug, the Reptile Gardens, Mount Rushmore, Deadwood, etc.) to Yellowstone Park (Old Faithful, sulfurous hot pools, souvenir shops, buffalo along the roads, etc.) to the Grand Tetons—Paul, Don and I bickering in the back seat all the way. The ending of this trip is indelibly inscribed in our family annals: We had pulled into a scenic overlook where in the distance, towering above the neighboring peaks, we could see the Holy Grail of our westward journey: the distinctive, snow-clad Grand Tetons in all their purple mountain majesty. Hushed by the magnificence of it all, as if in one of the great cathedrals of Europe, tourists pointed in awe, cameras clicked, and from the back seat one of us looked up from our comic books and asked, "When are we going home?"

"Right now!" Pop said, slamming his hands on the steering wheel, turning the car around, and speeding back to the flatlands of North Dakota and the amber waves of grain. It was the last major trip we took as a family.

Bored as we were at that age with natural beauty, the other sights on those family trips still stirred up a curiosity and a restlessness that left me vaguely discontented with home. We sure have nothing like The Foshay Tower in Grand Forks, I said to myself, or like the Minneapolis Lakers or the Museum of Science and Industry or Lake Michigan or *Mad* magazine. We have nothing like it in all of North Dakota. Why do we live here, I wondered, when we could live in a city with all that excitement?

Eventually I did move to "the cities." But there are days—more and more of them as I grow older—when I envy my contemporaries who have been content to stay put, to live out their lives where we were born. I've accepted that I can't be one of them, though, just as I've accepted that wherever I go, little bits of North Dakota will still be clinging to my shoes, and that however long I live, those puzzling memories of my father will linger among the others.

Despite my vague, incipient dissatisfaction with small town life and the monotony of the North Dakota landscape, there are elements of the prairie life that *did* have appeal, even in my adolescence. When fall arrived, Pop went into his gun closet and started getting out the gear—the shotguns and shells, the jackets and caps, the boots and the duck decoys—and Colonel, the golden retriever Pop had trained to do blind retrieves, even to break thin layers of ice if necessary to bring back ducks, began wriggling with anticipation. Merely opening that closet door did the trick, for both the dog and me: It released a flood of aromas—gunpowder, gun oil, the lingering smell of last year's kill, the little stalks of stubble or flax still clinging to pant cuffs—smells that revived trips of previous years. If our memories alone weren't enough, Pop had his hunting journals, a handwritten record of all the hunting trips he would take over thirty-some years. He could remind us how many ducks of each kind we'd shot on opening day on the slough west of Lakota, and what the weather was, or how many sharp-tailed grouse we'd gotten at Dunseith on the second weekend of October, who was with us and where we stayed.

To learn where the ducks were, in September Pop started making calls to other parts of the state—to a doctor he knew near Rolla, a filling station owner in Carrington, a farmer near Rollette—then we'd load the car on a Friday afternoon and set out for a long weekend. We'd spend the night in a small town motel, then get up in the early morning dark to be sure we were in position the moment we were allowed by law to shoot, a half hour before sunrise. The opening times for each day were given for Bismarck, so Pop measured our distance from the capitol and calculated that "a half hour before sunrise" meant we could begin shooting at, say, 6:17.

In our long underwear and layers of camouflage clothing we'd conceal our-selves at the edge of a slough and shiver in the early morning cold as we waited for light, warming ourselves with coffee or hot chocolate, listening to the ducks chattering among themselves out there in the blackness, peering through the dark for the first hints of dawn and signs of the day's weather. Colonel sat with us impatiently, barely able to control himself, whimpering and shivering not with cold but excitement.

At midday, congregating at the car for a tailgate picnic of sandwiches and Mom's homemade doughnuts, we'd recount our successes or failures of the morning—the easy shots missed, the hard shots made—and figure the number of ducks we'd need to reach our limit.

In the afternoons while the ducks were feeding in the fields, we peeled off the heavy, camouflage clothing and, in shirtsleeves, walked the stubble fields and hedgerows looking for sharp-tail grouse and Hungarian partridge or combed the cornfields for pheasants. Then in the late afternoons we'd pull on our camouflage clothing again and return to the sloughs, hoping to pick off a few more ducks as they flew back in for the night.

Our family albums hold numerous photos of these hunts; in the typical pic-ture, we're sitting on the tailgate of our red Chevy Bel Aire station wagon with family friends, usually other doctors from Pop's clinic, with numerous ducks or upland birds lying breast-up in neat rows at our feet.

There was a complex appeal for me in these hunting trips. Part of it was simply being outdoors in the broad, rural North Dakota landscape in fall, whatever the weather. Part of it was rising in the early morning dark and being at-large before the rest of the world (so many great enterprises—mountain climbs, or long journeys of any kind—call for getting up in the pre dawn hours); part of it was the smells of gunpowder and mucky slough bottoms, of homemade doughnuts and dusty fields of grain after the fall harvest, and the camaraderie and happiness that bubble up when people plunge into things that bring them pleasure.

Pop would take the birds to Mrs. Sawatsky's for cleaning, then wrap them carefully, label them and store them in the basement freezer, each one a time capsule transporting us back to a date and a place, each one rekindling the satisfaction of harvesting our own meal. On a Sunday evening in the cold of winter, Pop would build a fire in the fireplace, Mom would fix a dinner of roast duck and wild rice, and we'd eat in the living room in front of the fire.

"These are canvasback we shot that weekend at McVille," Pop might say. The mention of McVille and the sight, the smell, and the taste of the rich, dark brown meat stirred up a parade of memories.

"That's the weekend we got our limit by noon."

"And when Paul doubled on pintails."

"Wasn't that the trip that Colonel got into the box of doughnuts and finished them all?"

"Oops," someone would eventually say, carefully taking a small, lead pellet from his mouth. "Watch out for buckshot."

◆　　　◆　　　◆

It was during this junior high phase of my life, at age 15, that I formally entered the work force, albeit briefly. My place of employment was the Westward Ho Motel, the newest, fanciest motel in town, and my job there was the result of blatant nepotism, the manager being the husband of a second cousin. My job description was to do whatever the boss told me to do, which was varied, sometimes physically taxing, and sometimes downright disgusting. For 90 cents an hour, sometimes I pitched hay over newly-seeded patches of ground and dug post holes for a new fence, both under relentless summer heat; sometimes I worked in the sauna-hot laundry where I washed sheets and towels and lugged them over to the dryer; and sometimes I cleaned the guest rooms.

It was cleaning the guestrooms that provided another of those lurches and leaps in the process of growing up: the reminder that other families are different from mine. In our family we didn't leave behind soiled sheets; we didn't polish and shine our shoes with the motel towels; we didn't clean our shoes in the sink and leave behind large clods of mud, or spatter the sink with blood and leave it for someone else to clean up.

The pay, 90 cents an hour, was better than it had been in magazine sales and trapping, but after I'd earned enough to buy myself a new set of golf clubs, I retired from motel work and am grateful that I've never had to go back to it.

During these junior high years I began pulling away from my parents and taking trips on my own. In the summer of 1952, between our seventh and eighth grades, three of my school friends and I took a four day camping trip in a grove of cottonwoods at the western edge of town on the farm of our neighbors the Rays—land that is now a golf course. Our parents drove us to this not-very-distant site, and during our sojourn there they occasionally came back to re-supply us with food and water, but otherwise—to our amazement and delight—they left us alone. We slept in a musty canvas tent owned first by Pop's father, a tent that had lain unused in our attic for decades. We fixed our own meals around a wood fire—peanut butter and jelly sandwiches, hot dogs with baked beans, bacon and eggs—and we flaunted our freedom and independence by the liberal, indiscriminate use of obscenities and profanities.

"Don't just stand there, goddammit. Put some more wood on the fuckin' fire."

"Jesus, no! The fuckin' fire is too big already. You wanna burn the goddamned eggs?"

"You wanna cook the goddamned eggs yourself, just say so."

"Fuck you. Where's the salt and pepper? I just put it down a minute ago."

"You already put so much salt and pepper on the fuckin' eggs, nobody's gonna be able to eat 'em."

"That shows what the hell you know about cookin'. You just keep that bacon from burning to a fuckin' crisp, the way you burned it yesterday, and everything's gonna be just fine."

"Where the hell are the baked beans? Who the fuck's gonna cook the beans?"

"Baked beans for breakfast? Jesus Christ, who ever heard of baked beans for breakfast?"

"Damn right. It'll be the best fuckin' breakfast you ever had."

"Oh, yeh?"

"Fuckin' A."

"Who the hell swiped the ketchup?"

"*Ketchup?* It's *catsup*, fer crissakes, not fuckin' *ketchup*. And whadda ya want catsup for anyway?"

"Fer the fuckin' *eggs*, fer crissakes."

"Yer gonna put *catsup* on *eggs?* Jesus fuckin' Christ!"

"No, I'm gonna put *ketchup* on eggs, you dumb shit."

For our other amusements, we swam in the English Coulee nearby and, because we were still in the savage period called childhood, we snared gophers, using old pieces of twine we'd found nearby. We made nooses, placed them around the gopher holes, then gripped the opposite end of the twine, lay flat on the ground several feet away, and made low, whistling sounds. When a curious gopher poked his head out of the hole, we'd yank on the twine, snaring the gopher around the neck and jerking him through the air, then reel him in and finish him off with a gleeful stomp of the foot.

Later trips took us further and further from home, especially after we'd learned to drive. One summer—I'm jumping ahead a few years now—we camped on a hilltop overlooking Lake Marquette in Northern Minnesota. Another summer we camped along the Mississippi, and on another—our first canoe trip—we paddled the Upper Mississippi between Lake Bemidji and the river's source at Lake Itasca.

We took our last trip together in the summer of 1957, after our graduation from high school. Renting canoes, tents, and Duluth packs from an outfitter in Northern Minnesota, we paddled north for days, crossing the border into Canada's Quetico National Park and following the chains of lakes and portage trails on the greatest adventure of our lives. Hitherto abstinent, we packed along several cases of beer we'd bought illegally, stowing the bottles in our packs to keep them cold, and allotted ourselves two beers per person a day. At the end of a strenuous portage, we'd launch the canoes in the next lake and from the Duluth packs bring forth cold beers as our reward. Lying back in the canoe with the sun on our faces, sipping from the bottles, cooling our hands in the clear, deep waters of those Canadian lakes, it seemed impossible that anything could ever be better. (We hadn't tried sex yet; but even in spite of all we'd heard in locker rooms, it was hard to imagine that even sex could measure up to this.) With impressive self-restraint, some of us abstained on those tempting occasions, ensuring that on our last night together in the wilderness we'd have enough left to get delightfully, memorably drunk.

◆   ◆   ◆

In that three-year transition between elementary school and high school, I was becoming more aware of the wider world, even if only vaguely. I was aware of the election of Eisenhower and Nixon in '52 and, in '53, of the death of Stalin, the execution of spies Julius and Ethel Rosenberg, the successful testing of the Salk polio vaccine, the armistice in Korea, and the ongoing tests of nuclear bombs by the U.S. and the Soviet Union. Thanks to the black and white photographs in *Life* magazine, I was fuzzily aware of the nationwide concern about communism, the Army-McCarthy hearings, and the de-frocking of McCarthy in 1954. Even some of the less consequential events caught my attention—Edmund Hillary's ascent of Everest, Christine Jorgenson's sex-change operation, the emergence of Marilyn Monroe, and the sudden popularity of Bill Hailey's "Rock Around the Clock."

There were other significant events that never registered at all in the memory of an isolated teenager on the Northern Plains: the Supreme Court decision in 1954 to outlaw racial segregation in public schools, which simply had no relevance to a teenager in the racially monochromatic Red River Valley. And the defeat of the French by the Communists in Viet Nam—like Korea, Viet Nam was just another place we'd never heard of, and it certainly had nothing to do with us. The nationwide migration of city dwellers to the suburbs—one of the transforming events of American life in that century—was well underway, but that too was happening to other people in other places. Still not a reader, I never noticed new books like *The Catcher in the Rye, From Here to Eternity, The Caine Mutiny, Andersonville, The Man in the Gray Flannel Suit, The Old Man and the Sea,* and *Lolita.* And since we didn't have a television set in our house then—all my friends had TV before we did—I didn't yet understand the attraction of shows like "I Love Lucy," "Dragnet," "Lassie," and "Ozzie and Harriet."

Having been no more aware than I was of the important events of that time, I grew up thinking of the fifties as a dull decade, and it wasn't until many years later when I began reading twentieth century history that I came to see how wrong I'd been. Finally I came to recognize the complexity of that period and the swirl of social change that accompanied it, at least on the national level. But for my young friends and me, shielded as we were by our cultural and geographical isolation and by the myopia of the early teenage years, it was a just a simple, happy time.

For the young, blinded by self-centeredness, the wider world is dwarfed by an indulgence in having the right clothes and hairstyle, in being pimple free, in being cool. Still, while it isn't surprising that I was oblivious to Dienbienphu and Brown vs. the Board of Education, in retrospect I think I was also unaware of a profound change that *did* affect me personally.

Part of this change was my desperate desire to grow up, to be more like adults. That part I was aware of, even if in a fuzzy kind of way. The first sign for me was the pleasure I found in kissing Judy Loft and Karen Ray. The second came a year later when I discarded my fancy Schwinn bike for a Whizzer motorbike that went 30 miles per hour and advanced my independence by increasing my distance from home.

My interest in girls was nudged along by school dances held in the junior high gym that we'd decorated with streamers of crepe paper and where Coach Nelson led us through a highly stylized, completely asexual maneuver called "The Grand March." As silly as it felt to proceed through this formal ritual under the crisp hand signals of Mr. Nelson, a routine he conducted with funereal solemnity, it was easier and more comfortable than dancing with an actual girl, one-on-one and face to face, where you had no one to tell you what to do and when to do it. Dancing, it seemed to me, unlike sex, was suspiciously illogical, "a perpendicular expression of a horizontal desire," as G. B. Shaw called it.

Yet, like religion at that stage of my life, it seemed to be one of those institutions that must be endured. So when the first dance loomed before me in those junior high years, I had to recruit someone safe—Susie Barnes, the girlfriend of my friend "Durd" Sollom—to give me a lesson, which she conducted in her living room. Short, pert, dark-haired Susie put a 45 rpm record on the phonograph, and while Kitty Kallen sang "Little Things Mean a Lot" she steered me patiently through the two-step. By the time Doris Day had finished "Secret Love," I figured I knew enough to get by. Still, when Susie and I were coincidentally chosen king and queen of the ninth grade Valentine's Dance, rather than circulate as beaux of the ball I preferred to seclude myself in the concession stand and dispense soft drinks and sugared doughnuts. At a dance, I was no more at ease than I'd been in kindergarten or in church, venues that had only helped to heighten the appeal of solitude.

By my final year at South I had a steady girlfriend with whom I spent many evenings side by side on her living room couch not knowing what to say—it was becoming clear that I had no more future as a great lover than I had as a salesman or a wilderness trapper—but conversation was far less interesting than kissing anyway, which, when her parents weren't home, took place in an increasingly horizontal mode. ("Oh Lord," as St. Augustine said, "help me to be pure, but not yet.") A year later, with my driver's license in hand, I abandoned my motorbike and greatly expanded not only my range of mobility but my opportunities for such pursuits.

I think it was about this time that Pop called Paul and me in for The Talk. We had been upstairs in our room studying one night when he knocked on our door and beckoned us downstairs for some reason he didn't immediately disclose. He ushered us into his knotty pine den where Paul and I sat side by side on the couch while Pop sat across from us in his upholstered chair. The topic, it turned out, was the penis and the vagina and how they fit together in the mechanics of sex. Unlike the dangers of the river, it was a topic that didn't lend itself well to his empirical method of instruction. Still, in his clinical presentation of the topic he was quite accurate and admirably thorough, I thought, even though the information was somewhat redundant by that point in our adolescence. I was simultaneously amused by his awkwardness and impressed by his doing his duty, even though he didn't have his heart in it any more than he had in our earlier instruction in religion.

In our fascination with sex, my friends and I talked a lot about going all the way and we speculated seriously about whether so-and-so really put out or was only a prick tease, and one or two of my friends made a show of carrying a rubber or two in their billfolds. But it was only our hormones talking. Everyone knew that if you got a girl pregnant you had to marry her. So I suspect that 99 percent of us were virgins when we finished high school, the exception being a sultry classmate who suddenly disappeared and was gone for the rest of her junior year, abortion being illegal and dangerous and therefore rare. (The most surprising part of this event was that our chief suspect as the impregnator was a boy we might have voted Least Likely to Get Laid but who suddenly took on much greater stature in our eyes.)

◆   ◆   ◆

It was the opportunity to drive that most dramatically signaled the end of one stage of our lives and the start of another, and it's understandable, I suppose, that at that point we looked forward rather than back: to high school sports with much classier uniforms; to night football games at the University stadium, under the lights and with much bigger crowds; to basketball games in the high school gym, with a band and real cheerleaders. And for me, to another season of track and a good chance of winning a medal at the state meet.

These were the important things to us then, the changes we *were* aware of. But what is more interesting to me now is not what lay ahead of us as we hurtled into our teenage years but what we so mindlessly left behind. In that transitional phase of junior high, what was changing most about our lives was our forms of play. We were, as I said, working hard to grow up, a herky-jerky process fueled largely by glands, and growing up meant turning our backs on the river.

I didn't have the words then to explain what the river meant; it was simply a given, something everyone ought to have in his own backyard. Now I see that for those of us who lived along it, the river was the first great frontier in our lives, a sinuous ribbon of unsettled space running north and south as far as we dared to go, or as far as our parents let us. It was a world of the unknown, a land of mystery and danger. It invited exploration and discovery, holding the same allure for us then that the great Western frontier held for other Americans in the previous century. For eight to 10 precious years in our young lives—in an era before sports camps and computer camps, before television and institutionalized play—before we were seduced by what we thought were more grownup pursuits, the river was the main attraction in our lives, an everyday circus of adventure. And in our thoughtful and vulnerable childhood, it went without saying that adventure was among the necessities of life.

But as adolescence seized control of us, we gradually, unwittingly became susceptible to the myth that adventure is more appropriately the province of children. A small handful of us tried to sustain and nurture that yearning through our summer camping trips and our voyages by canoe, but eventually we too turned away from the river and everything it represented. We worked hard to grow up and move on. Erratically, often comically, we tried to behave like adults as we drifted through high school, then college. Sooner or later we succeeded, taking our places behind desks, in cities, having abandoned the river and all that it signified. Most of us never returned, never even looked back. But while we were there, it was an enviable time and place.

8

[The remembering self] has the temperament
of a librarian, a keeper of memory's most
important archives…fastidious…guarding its
original records and trying to keep them pristine.

White Gloves: How We Create Ourselves Through Memory—
John Kotre

In the postwar years, we Americans became unprecedentedly rich.

With disposable personal income shooting up dramatically, we had a lot of money to spend and an increasing number of things to spend it on—new homes and new appliances to put in them, new automobiles, new television sets. (Five-sixths of all television sets in the world belonged to Americans.) Television created a new era in advertising, teasing us with new products and enticing us with visions of ease and luxury. More and more of us had leisure time for listening to records, for ball games, movies, concerts and theaters, for hunting and fishing. By the fifties, every third American owned a car, and there was an average of one television set and three radios per household. We were wallowing in prosperity.

Mom and Pop were never extravagant or ostentatious—extravagance and ostentation violated the North Dakota code—but they rode high on this wave of affluence too; as soon as the war was over and auto manufacturers were building cars again instead of military trucks and tanks, they bought a new car to replace the prewar Dodge with the wooden bumpers. Then they started hunting for vacation property on the same shore of Minnesota's Lake Bemidji where Pop had spent his primitive summers as a boy.

Most of the lakeshore had been developed in the thirty-some intervening years, so, with few lots left, they looked first at cabins for sale, even trying out a few during summer vacations to see how they fit. One was a small, dark, ramshackle dwelling with a loft accessible only by a flimsy staircase that could be raised and lowered like a Venetian blind. The other—my preference—was a larger, more substantial log house that looked more as a lake cabin should. But Mom and Pop finally decided to build a cabin of their own on Lavinia beach, choosing a 100-foot lot covered mostly with young oaks with a few mature red and white pines, and in 1948 the construction began.

The finished cabin was unpretentious—it had a living room and kitchen with knotty pine walls, three small bedrooms, and a bath—and in those early years the furniture was rustic, like everything else about the place. In terms of the household conveniences of the time, it was a charming step backwards. We had an icebox instead of a refrigerator, with ice delivery twice a week. There was no phone, no washer or dryer. Mom took the laundry into town or washed it in a portable machine that fit in the kitchen sink, then hung it on a clothesline outside. She washed dishes by hand and stacked them on open shelves above the kitchen sink. We made our breakfast toast in one of those old electric toasters with the drop-down sides, which even then were starting to show up in antique stores. Mom and Pop didn't subscribe to a newspaper at the lake; if anyone wanted news of the outside world, we had a small radio, but we never used it. When we needed heat, we built a fire in the fireplace. Storms off the lake blew rainwater in through the loose-fitting windows. Sometimes bats got in and nested in a little-used water pitcher high on a kitchen shelf, and one winter, chipmunks left a cache of acorns in a pair of boots in the coat closet. In this primitive simplicity, the difference between indoors and outdoors was minimal. It was my childhood Elysium.

Soon after school was out, like so many other Upper Midwesterners we started packing for "the lake," which in the parlance of the Upper Midwest could mean any one of Minnesota's supposed 10,000, then loaded the car and headed east on the interminable two-hour drive to Bemidji. Leaving Grand Forks, we passed first through the broad, treeless, monotonously flat potato fields of Northeastern Minnesota and—except for Crookston, a county seat—through a succession of small towns of small consequence, none more than 1,600 people even today. ("What do people *do* here anyway," I asked every time.) After 70 miles we left behind the potato fields and the black, rich earth of the Red River Valley and entered a region with sandy soil producing little but a scattered forest of jack pine, poplar and birch. Even if I'd been blindfolded, I'd have known when I reached that point: I could *smell* it—the rich, sweet green smell of pine forest—and then I knew we were close. When we finally reached the town of Bemidji, we turned onto the highway that starts around the lake. In those days the highway later turned into two-lane gravel and the two-lane gravel later dwindled to one-lane dirt, and in another mile we were there, for the summer. Or I should say Mom and we kids were. Pop and the other Grand Forks fathers who had cabins at the lake worked in town during the week and—except for his vacations—came to the lake just for the weekends.

Out the front door we had a sandy beach and the lake, seven miles long and three miles across. Out the back door and across the road was a marsh where ducks nested in spring, where red wing black birds trilled in the day and frogs croaked loudly at night, and on either side of the marsh was pine forest threaded with trails. It was a world of new smells—the pine forest, of course, but also the smells of fresh, clear water, of dried seaweed on the beach, of wood smoke coming from chimneys on cool mornings. And new sounds—ducks quacking from the marsh, waves slapping the shore, outboard motors droning from the lake. As if growing up along a river for nine months of the year weren't privilege enough, I had the lake for the other three.

Part of the luxury was a whole new batch of friends. There were as many as 12 other children within playing distance along the beach, both boys and girls; it didn't seem to matter that there was a gap of four or five years between the youngest (me) and the oldest. And our childhood activities at the lake were completely different from our games at home.

In our first years we were satisfied to play in the shallow water near the shore and make sandcastles on the beach, and sometimes our parents drove us to stables west of Bemidji where we took trail rides through the woods. When we learned to swim, we rowed our small aluminum boat to the diving raft, then swam toward shallower water until we could feel the bottom, hoping to avoid the slimey, tickly feeling of weeds.

We organized our own badminton and horseshoe tournaments, and on rainy days or in the evenings we played outdoor games like Shipwreck, and indoor games like Monopoly or Scrabble, or card games like Fish and Pig or, when we were older, Whist or Hearts.

One day we might hike a mile to Rocky Point, a high sandy bluff overlooking the north end of the lake. At the top of the bluff was a small open field where we could get a good run before leaping out into the air, then landing on the sandy slope and sliding down to the boulder-strewn beach below. On another we might hike the dirt road through the woods to the railroad tracks and put keys or coins on the rails, or go to the shed-like Lavinia station and flag down the once-a-day passenger train for the seven-mile ride into town for an afternoon movie.

When we were a little older we went to the Paul Bunyan Playhouse, a summer stock theater at the north end of the lake where I saw my first real play—Agatha Christie's *Ten Little Indians*—or to town for the start of the Canoe Derby, an annual, 225 mile race down the Mississippi to Minneapolis, or for the Fourth of July festivities, including the annual water-ski show where skiers skied barefoot, built human pyramids, and soared off ramps, then did helicopter spins in the air.

These water-ski shows were an inspiration to me. In our earliest years at the lake, the boats along our beach were small and the motors not powerful enough to pull skiers, but gradually the boats got bigger and the motors more powerful, and then water-skiing became one of our favorite pastimes.

It didn't take me long to advance from two skis to one, then move on to foolhardy stunts like skiing at night, when there was a risk of hitting floating objects in the lake, and putting the tow rope around my head.

But the water ski-shows exposed me to legitimate tricks that I was eager to pull off myself. When I was still pretty small and light, I skied with a neighbor—a man who had an inboard speedboat and who was intrigued with the idea of pyramids. We figured out how I could ski alongside him, kick off one ski, put my free foot into the cupped hand near his waist, then step out of the other ski and end up sitting on his shoulders.

When I got older and too heavy for that trick, I skied with a friend who bought a trick ski that enabled us to do 360 degree turns, and after that I learned how to do jumps off a ramp. I never tried the helicopter spin—you hit the ramp with the rope curled halfway around your waist; then when you've left the ramp, you let go with one hand and find yourself doing a full turn in the air before hitting the water—but I figured I was good enough to apply for a summer job with the professional troupe that performed at the annual Fourth of July show on the waterfront. I couldn't think of anything better than traveling from town to town and skiing with those beautifully tanned blondes who toured the country each summer. So I sent numerous applications to the Tommy Bartlett Water-Ski Show in Wisconsin Dells, Wisconsin, but never got a reply. Another disappointment, another promising career stillborn.

At least once a summer our entertainment came in the guise of a storm off the lake. Some of these storms lasted as long as a day, bringing high waves that crashed on our shore and sometimes pounded the underside of our dock and pushed it off kilter. When a storm brought rain—we could see it coming across the lake, starting from the far shore—we rushed to the linen closet for towels to mop up the water that seeped through the loose-fitting windows and puddled on the living room floor. In one nighttime storm with both wind and rain, the power went out, and as we were mopping up in the dark, a flash of lightening illuminated the turbulent scene outside: trees lashed by the wind, pools of water on the lawn, and our aluminum lawn furniture flying past the windows.

When the wind finally subsided we went down to the beach to see what the waves had brought in. Once in a while there was a boat that had broken loose from its buoy across the lake, and occasionally beach toys—an air mattress, a beach ball, a child's sand pail. There were always ridges of wet seaweed which we raked into piles and lugged across the road to the marsh before it started to rot and lure sand flies, and scores of dead whitefish and suckers which we buried deep in the sand.

Summer at the lake was a parade of sensual pleasures, and one of the simplest was the short walk down the road to Tillie's and Manda's store—not much more than a shack—where two little antique ladies tended a limited inventory of candy, soft drinks, dust-covered canned goods, and homemade doughnuts. On a hot day, with the sun beating on my back and the grasshoppers buzzing in the tall grass along the road, it was delicious to anticipate the Popsicle or cold soft drink I could buy for a nickel at Tillie and Manda's. On Saturday mornings when they prepared bread and pies on special order, the fragrance of fresh baked goods spread up and down the beach, mingling with the smells of the pine forest and wood smoke.

One of our childhood activities, a nocturnal one, certainly imprudent and ultimately destructive, was to post a detour sign on the narrow dirt road and deflect drivers down a single track side road that came to a dead end a hundred yards into the woods. We painted what we considered an official-looking sign, black with white letters, and while the letters were still wet we sprinkled them with salt in an ineffectual attempt to make them reflective. We hung the sign on a clothesline rope that we stretched across the road—a clothesline rope we borrowed from O.J. Barnes, a nearly blind old man who lived nearby—then concealed ourselves in the woods and waited. Eventually a car would approach, see the sign and slow down, then turn hesitatingly onto the side road. When his taillights disappeared around the corner, we'd emerge from our cover, take down the sign, then hide in the woods again, snickering and congratulating ourselves on our cleverness. Within just a few minutes the driver would reach the dead end, probably scratch his head, then turn around and come back out to the main road and, seeing no sign, continue on his way—deeply mystified, we were sure—and we'd laugh and congratulate ourselves all over again. The following morning, before re-stringing the clothesline we'd borrowed from the nearly blind owner, we'd snicker with amusement as he fruitlessly pawed the air in search of the familiar place to hang his laundry.

This little game gave us many evenings of juvenile entertainment over several summers; but as the years passed, our narrow dirt road became two-lane gravel and finally blacktop, and instead of creeping along at 10 to 15 miles per hour, cars sped by at 30 to 40. One night a driver didn't see our sign in time, probably didn't see it at all, didn't even slow down until he hit it. We heard the shattering of a headlight and the screech of tires on blacktop. All in all, it was reminiscent of the crab apple incident: In the long, universal tradition of childhood, we failed to imagine the danger in our foolishness until the consequences hit us in the face.

That change in the road that summer was symptomatic of more widespread change that happened more gradually over the years, a move away from the primitive quality that had made our lake world so attractive to me in the beginning. The widening road that became blacktop and that brought faster traffic and more noise was just the first step. That transformation was reflected too in our change of address. When we first settled on Lavinia, our mailing address was simply Route 5, Bemidji, Minnesota. Mail would reach us even without the "Route 5." But a few years later we became Route 5, Box 69, and ultimately our road was even given a name—Lavinia Road N.E.—and we were assigned a house number and ultimately a zip code. We were getting less and less rural.

Other changes were instigated by Mom and Pop themselves, and some even by us children. Our first watercraft, for example, was a narrow, twelve-foot aluminum boat small enough for us children to row. (Part of the fun was sliding the boat down to the water in the morning, finding the leeches underneath, sprinkling them with salt, and watching them writhe in agony.) But as we grew older we weren't content to row anymore; we agitated for a motor, and gradually we wanted bigger motors and bigger boats so we could keep up with our friends, so we could water-ski without relying on the boats of friends and neighbors.

While these changes were going on outdoors, others were going on indoors. Over time, Mom and Pop got rid of the cheap, grass rugs in the living room and installed wall to wall carpeting throughout the cabin. Over time, they put in electric wall heaters, which relieved us of the joy of building a fire in the morning. They installed new countertops and new cupboards in the kitchen and bought a new refrigerator and a freezer (they had long ago abandoned the icebox). They put insulation in the ceiling and installed tighter windows so we could use the cabin well into the fall. They hauled in some black dirt, scattered some grass seed, and started a lawn, which meant we also needed a power mower. Finally they did what I'd thought they would never do at the lake—I thought they would sell the cabin first—they bought a large, color TV. Our lakeside residence no longer had the charm of a cabin; it had degenerated into a house.

And so it went—our desire for convenience and comfort, for what we believed to be progress, forever at odds with my longing for the primitive and the simple. When we choose the whir of the electric heater over the crackle and aroma of the birch fire, when we put our faith in the outboard motor and give up the quiet exertion of rowing, when we drove to the store for the newspaper and renounced the adventure of a morning walk, I was surely more comfortable but certainly not more content. We merely intensified my longing for the primitive.

But of all the changes that took place there over the years, none caused more controversy in our family than the installation of a phone. For years Pop didn't want one. So while all our neighbors were dialing away and transacting their daily business with the help of this simple convenience, we went without. The *avant garde* in our family pointed out the awkwardness of having to go to neighbors to make a call. "What do you think the neighbors are saying," they'd ask. "'When is that cheapskate Woutat going to spring for a few bucks and put in a phone of his own?'" The holdouts saw the phone as a battering ram against our fortress of privacy and quiet. "Put in a phone and it'll be ringing all the time. It'll be the end of the cabin as we know it."

We resolved the dilemma by having a phone but pretending we didn't. It was mounted on the kitchen wall behind a curtain where it was invisible, and it had a switch that allowed us to shut off the bell so we couldn't hear it. We could make calls in emergencies but we wouldn't give out the number, and guests, seeing no phone, would continue to believe we didn't have one.

Our naiveté was short-lived; soon we were making and receiving calls right and left. It was just too inconvenient to leave our city habits behind.

Summers at the lake weren't always an idyll. There were bouts with poison ivy and swimmer's itch; there were black flies that bit us until early July and mosquitoes that pestered us throughout the summer; at night we picked engorged wood ticks from our bodies and held them over a flame 'til they popped. But a benevolent memory pushes all that aside and what I remember more are the simple pleasures that in retrospect seem more like luxuries: lying on the dock at night and seeing the northern lights and more stars than I'd seen anywhere else; catching fireflies in a jar and marveling at their mysterious glow as I fell asleep to the chorus of frogs from the marsh across the road; rising early, building a fire to warm the cabin, then stealing across to my bird watching perch on the edge of the marsh to catch a glimpse of migrating warblers; then, with a couple of species added to my life list, returning to the cabin for a breakfast of pan-fried walleyes freshly caught.

But there was something else underlying all that I've told about so far, something more elemental. When the two-hour drive from Grand Forks was over and we'd moved into the cabin for the summer, Mom and Pop were mysteriously transformed into different people—lighter, more buoyant, quicker to laugh, slower to snap. Mom laughed more at the lake, and Pop too was more relaxed. It happened to other adults too. The lake was a different world with different rules; we children could stay out later at night and answer less for our whereabouts. Up and down the beach there was a perceptible letting down of old social poses and props, a discarding of the more formal rituals of home and work. The adults we called Mr. and Mrs. Thompson at home were Loyde and Ethel at the lake. The parents had parties more often, were ready to kick up their heels, to drink and sing late into the night. (They didn't know that while they were entertaining themselves indoors, sometimes they were entertaining their children as well. Concealed in the darkness outside, we watched through the windows as these otherwise-formal adults—these people we'd thought of as old and stiff—burst forth in song, Indian wrestled on the floor, or gamboled with lampshades on their heads.)

When I reached my high school years, the lake became my summer training ground for football and track. I dug a pit in the lawn and filled it with sand to practice the high jump and long jump, and I did long solitary runs on the back roads in the woods where the only sounds were my own breathing and the occasional squawk of blue jays in the oaks. On other days, to build leg strength, I ran in knee-deep water or ran the sandy beach where I hurdled docks, and with these summer workouts I was more fit than I'd ever been.

One morning, apparently full of myself and probably having been prattling obnoxiously about my dazzling future as a runner with Olympic potential, I was forced to reassess my prospects. While I was carrying on, Pop was lying on the living room couch reading his latest *Sports Afield.* After a while he couldn't take it any more.

"I don't think you're so damned fast," he said from behind his magazine.

"Is that a challenge?"

"Put your money where your mouth is." He wasn't smiling.

The next thing I knew, Pop and I were walking out to the road behind the cabin with Paul coming along as starter. Already dressed for my daily workout, I was wearing shorts and running shoes, but Pop had on long pants and his street shoes. While Paul and I stood waiting, he marked off a starting line, then meticulously paced off 100 yards. "Is this really happening?" I wondered.

We went into the starter's crouch, Paul gave us the "ready, set, go," and the race was on.

Sprinting was not my strength, I admit. I'd never broken 11 seconds in the hundred. But I wasn't slow either, and besides, I was 17 and fit from all that distance training in the woods and the beach running in water and sand. Pop was 51 and balding; he hadn't trained since high school; and was wearing long pants and street shoes. In spite of it all, the embarrassing, humiliating truth is that he left me in his dust. When the race was over, I stood there on the road trying to figure out what to make of this strange event while Pop started back to the cabin and his *Sports Afield*, the corners of his mouth turning up slightly in the hint of a grin.

It had been another of his lessons without words, like the lesson years earlier with the stones and the river. But this one left me with unanswered questions. Whom did he intend this lesson to benefit, I wonder? It might have done wonders for him, might have proved his fitness and superior speed and given his ego a boost, but it didn't do much for me. If it did nothing else, it *should* have caused me to question my future in track. What high school runner with Olympic promise gets beaten by a balding 51-year old in street shoes who hasn't trained for decades? But it didn't. It just mortified me, and it made me wonder why a father would do such a thing to his son.

All in all though, remembered from the palliative distance of years, summer at the lake was like a good book I never wanted to end. But then it's late August, school approaches; the nights get cooler, the sumac turns red, and ducks start to gather on the lake for their fall migration. When that happens, families prepare for migrations of their own. It's abrupt and unsettling: By the end of Labor Day weekend, the shades are drawn and the doors locked, most of the docks are taken out and stacked on the lawns, the boats and picnic tables and lawn furniture and charcoal grills are stored in the garage, and once again the beach is forlorn, dormant, haunted by ghosts and soon to be encrusted in snow and ice.

We went through this annual fall ritual for almost forty years, until Pop died and Mom sold the cabin because she couldn't stand being there without him, and now it lives only in fading photographs and these dimming scraps of memory.

9

We are well-advised to keep on nodding terms
with the people we used to be, whether we find them
attractive company or not. Otherwise they turn up
unannounced and surprise us, come hammering on the
mind's door at 4 am of a bad night and demand to know
who deserted them, who betrayed them, who is going
to make amends. We forget all too soon the things
we thought we could never forget.

"On Keeping a Notebook"—
Joan Didion

Having been a high school teacher in the 1960's and 1970's, a period of angst and long-haired rebellion and drug use and protests against racism, the draft, the Vietnam war, and other forms of injustice both real and imagined, it's hard not to look back on my own high school years in the 1950's as anything but comically serene. Between the 1963 assassination of President Kennedy and our extrication from Vietnam 10 years later, the guiding principle of many young people was to challenge everything, preferably loudly and angrily and sometimes destructively. But as high school students in the fifties, we were not marked by a burning social conscience or an eager intellect. The curse of our decade was that there was so little encouragement to innovate, to think originally, to challenge and probe, to mess with the god of conformity. Individualism, that long-touted hallmark of the American character, was conspicuously dormant in that era, the governing values instead being conformity, respectability, politeness, security, and the blind acceptance of inherited wisdom. We were children of Ozzie and Harriet.

So in 1954 when I started Central High School, the same school Pop attended 35 years earlier, there wasn't much to deflect me from my attentions to social life and sports. My classes certainly didn't. At 15, almost 16, schoolwork was just busy-work I did while thinking about friends and girls and sports. That I passed through this institution on the honor roll probably says less about my ability, interest, and diligence than about my teachers' expectations of me. Except for

World History, Chemistry and Physics, little thinking was required, nor were foreign languages—"Who needs a foreign language anyway? Or art? How can anyone make a living in art?" There was little emphasis on writing and there was no evidence that creativity was either encouraged or prized. In English, a novice teacher who didn't know any better expected me to observe fine distinctions between words, and to this strange expectation—he must have been a spiritual descendent of my great-grandfather McIntosh—I responded with puzzled disbelief. If I was assigned homework, it was minimal and I did it dutifully. Given my obeisance to the governing values of the time, my disinclination to ask troublesome questions, to challenge and probe, I suspect that even though I wasn't very stimulating to teach, I was certainly easy to manage, and my teachers seemed satisfied with that.

It seems consistent that my report cards show A's in "Deportment" and absolutely no tardiness in three years; I was a model for my time. Ozzie and Harriet would have been proud.

The goal of being "well-rounded"—it was often held up to us as one of the noblest achievements of all—seemed worthy to me, but I gave a narrow interpretation to the term. When it might have nudged me toward school plays and the study of Latin, say, I tended to stick with what felt safe, which meant clubs where I could associate with fellow members of the fraternity of jocks.

Given my lifelong hesitancy to assert myself, it's strange to remember that I was elected an officer of various clubs, a role I wore like an ill-fitting suit, and I can theorize only that because I aged early and looked older than my contemporaries—I was shaving daily by this time—I inadvertently had an aura of maturity and self-confidence I never felt, and thus was expected to lead, just as tall people were expected to play basketball and fat people to be jolly. So as a senior I was nominated for president of the student council. Rather than decline a role I knew wouldn't fit, I drifted passively through the process, basking in the flattery of the nomination; but when I won I had surprisingly little idea how to play the part, even though I'd been in the organization for two years already and had been vice-president just the year before.

In most schools, certainly in mine, these organizations were basically impotent, so after scrambling to learn *Robert's Rules of Order*, I didn't do much but preside over meetings at which nothing happened but the adherence to parliamentary rules. Like the Japanese tea ceremony, it was an eminent illustration of form over substance. In my only effort to accomplish something—a solution to the lack of parking space for students—I was devastatingly unsuccessful. I rode to school with Noodle and Bear Grinnell in their orange and black Mercury, and when we got downtown, like our classmates who drove we had trouble finding a place to park. So with the full weight of my lofty office behind me, I went to the principal's office where, wearing my best manners, I politely asked for his support when I petitioned the police department to reserve a few spaces outside the school for students.

I hadn't confronted a principal since my meeting with Mr. Loomer at Lincoln Elementary, but it seemed that in the intervening six years principals hadn't become any less intimidating. Lawrence Hansen was a tall, stern, thin man with gray, immaculately combed hair and a patrician's bearing. Behind his back we called him "Gobbleneck" because of his wattle and the great distance between his shoulders and his head. His desk was a reflection of the man—large, immaculate, with phone, books, and papers neatly in place.

He didn't ask me to sit down—Mr. Loomer at least offered that; he didn't invite any chitchat, didn't ask how things were going, didn't probe the president of the student government for intelligence about student concerns. He just listened impatiently with a faraway look in his eyes, then—with no questions, no discussion, no apparent deliberation—he delivered his abrupt and monosyllabic reply. If he'd elaborated—if he'd argued that students weren't *supposed* to drive to school, that in *his* day they walked or rode horses, etc., etc.—his response would have been less surprising.

Student leaders of the seventies might have seized the principal's office in protest and chained themselves to the radiator until their demands were met. I just left, as politely as I'd come.

The experience reaffirmed the feeling that I was sadly miscast in this leadership role, didn't have the forcefulness or self-confidence to pull it off, despite what my contemporaries might have thought. It called for a more public person than I, or for someone who could for the occasion at least *pretend* to enjoy the limelight and take advantage of the position to bring about some good. So when my term of office was over, it was a wonderful relief to no longer have to feel like a fraud, to slip back into the single identity of runner where I felt qualified and safe.

Still, like my earlier excursions in religion and trapping and magazine sales, it showed me who I was *not*, and so was a useful part of my childhood. Sooner or later, if only by process of elimination, I'd somehow figure out who I was, would create a self that felt like a good fit. (A few years later the role of follower became as unattractive as the role of leader, so the only position left was that of detached observer, a role I have filled comfortably ever since.)

Through my high school years I never thought of exploring the world outside my cozy fraternity of jocks, which identified itself by our letter jackets, which we wore all the time, and our letter sweaters, which we wore on game days, and by a group called the Lettermen's Club. I don't remember that the Lettermen's Club did anything but elect officers and hold meetings at which nothing happened; we certainly didn't use our influence for the betterment of either the school or the community. Its chief attraction was its exclusivity and its capacity to enforce our identity as athletes.

Since our classes and school organizations made so few demands on us, my athletic friends and I had plenty of time to play poker and watch television—professional football, westerns like "Have Gun, Will Travel," crime shows like "Dragnet," and sitcoms like "The Honeymooners." Sometimes we went to sports events at the University. When new car models came out in the fall, we went to the showrooms ostensibly to behold the automotive changes—the introduction of Ford's new Thunderbird and the ill-omened Edsel, the new Chrysler with the push button transmission, and the proliferation of vehicular chrome—but really to eat the free doughnuts. We stopped at the newsstand to ogle the centerfolds in a new magazine called *Playboy* and we dropped in at the soda fountain for cherry cokes and glazed doughnuts. On winter nights we cruised the gravel roads outside of town with a .22 rifle and a spotlight, illegally shining for jackrabbits. Friday nights, dressed in our white bucks and the fashion colors of the time—pink and charcoal gray—our glossy, duck tail haircuts fixed in place with Brylcreme and our crew cuts by Butch Wax, we went to the "Y" and danced to the recorded voices of The Crew Cuts singing "Earth Angel" and Elvis singing "Love Me Tender," then to a drive-in for burgers and malts and fries, exotic foods like pizzas and tacos having not hit town yet.

If you wanted tranquil seas for your high school years, the fifties was the place to be. The economic prosperity allowed us comfortable lives and, the Korean War being over, we had no fear of the draft. (An exception was the Suez crisis in the fall of 1956 when for a few anxious weeks I felt the real fear that war might catapult me suddenly from high school to Egypt where I'd be brandishing a rifle instead of a diploma.) Beer was easily available, we heard; you just found a drunk who for a couple of dollars would buy you a sixpack. But as clean-cut athletes my friends and I adhered to the code of abstinence. We'd heard of marijuana but shunned it as we did alcohol. (Films like "Reefer Madness" proved it would drive us insane, just as wearing a cap indoors would cause baldness and masturbation would make us go blind.) Heroin and cocaine didn't exist for us, nor certainly did any of their more modern variants. There was a booming market in prescription tranquilizer sales in the fifties, but the users were all adults. There was also a booming market for religion in those days too, with church construction and church attendance at record heights.

In that faraway world, families could live well on just one income. All stores were closed on Sunday, so there wasn't much to do after church but eat Sunday dinner and watch professional football. At gas stations, uniformed attendants routinely cleaned your windshield and checked your oil and tires. Elevators—even in Grand Forks—were operated by humans, always wearing white gloves. Mail was delivered two times a day, six days a week. All in all, there has probably never been an easier, more pleasurable time to be an American or to be young. The code of conformity and respectability, the moral strictures of our Scandinavian-Lutheran climate, the unquestioned faith that all wrongs could be righted, the conviction that America was the greatest place on earth—all of these encased me in a cocoon of security and complacency and ensured that my cruise through adolescence was untroubled by the turbulence of social change.

Not everyone was at home in the fifties, of course. A liberal like Norman Mailer found it "one of the worst decades in the history of man." There certainly was a dark side to it. The Soviets, led by Kruschev—the man who later threatened to bury the U.S.—had just detonated their own hydrogen bomb and pushed the arms race to ever more frightening level, squashed a democratic revolution in Hungary, and were on the verge of beating us into space with their 1957 launch of Sputnik. Communists were expanding their influence in Southeast Asia, and rebels were warring with French colonists in Algeria. So the feeling of security at home was offset a little by growing insecurity in other parts of the world—including elsewhere in the U.S. where juvenile delinquency was becoming a national problem and where gun-carrying Federal troops were forcing racial integration of Arkansas schools. The schizophrenic element of the time was reflected in the fact that two of our favorite singers were the wholesomely conformist, white buck-shod, squeaky clean Christian Pat Boone and the greasy, longhaired, hip-gyrating rebel Elvis Presley, whom the Ed Sullivan show would televise only from the waist up and whom a female fan described as "one big hunk of forbidden fruit." Conservative George Will didn't like the decade much more than Mailer. As he put it retrospectively, the trouble with the fifties was that they were pregnant with the sixties. But in our self-centered adolescence and the security of our geographical isolation, it was easy to think of the world as a tranquil pond un-rippled by inconsistency or disorder.

One of the regrettable facts of our high school years was the impossibility of boys and girls to simply be friends. The differences between us were just too vast.

The boys-will-be-boys ethic permitted us to take part in sports, be elected school leaders, consider careers in law, science, medicine, business, and politics, and lust after girls. The girls-will-be-girls model required that they be unquestionably moral, that they defer to boys, and that they not take part in such unfeminine activities as sports, which might cause them to sweat and would presumably sabotage their reproductive systems and jeopardize their future as bearers of children. They were allowed to play basketball, but only in gym class, and only half-court. If they didn't want to grow up to be mothers, they could be teachers, nurses, secretaries, or airline stewardesses. While boys were predatory creatures who looked on girls largely as objects of sexual desire, girls were expected to sustain a radiance of detached purity, as if mindful of our expectation that on their wedding nights they would still be undefiled, an expectation comically and illogically at odds with our unflagging wish to get laid. So a constant tension existed between the sexes then, a boy plotting how far he could go, a girl wondering how far she should let him. It was a game that made friendship impossible, that precluded a luxury enjoyed now by our daughters and sons: the chance for boys and girls to know one another as friends, without the hindering, seemingly inevitable roles of predator and prey. With no sisters, it would have been nice to be able to have a friend who was also a girl.

But the most important business of school for most of my friends and me was sports, starting with football practice in August. At five foot-eight and 125 pounds, I was not a human battering ram, but I liked the camaraderie of sports, even football, so I came home early from those delicious summers at the lake and showed up eagerly for pre-season practice in the burdensome heat of late summer. We donned our armor and our football spikes in the school locker room, then walked to the practice field adjacent to the Chiefs' ballpark, a route that took us across the railroad tracks. If a train were passing by, we saw no reason to wait, preferring to grab hold of a moving car, hoist ourselves up, cross between cars, and hop down on the other side.

I was on the B squad as a sophomore but in the following year moved up to the varsity, which—according to our national ritual—played its games on Friday nights under the lights, in our case at the University stadium. For those having a stake in this ubiquitous fall pageant, it's an event filled with magic and drama and hope. And for those at the center of all this attention, those for whom the bands play and the fans and cheerleaders cheer and the sportswriters write—for most of them anyway—it's the epitome of childhood glory.

Too small, my speed diminished by the accumulated weight of shoulder pads, rib pads, hip pads, thigh pads, and helmet, I never found that glory in football after the ninth grade. But I stubbornly stuck with the sport, and as token thanks for my loyalty, the coach assigned me to return the kickoff in our first game of our senior year. Standing near the goal line in my maroon jersey and silver pants, with the school band playing the school song, with several thousand fans and a couple of prospective girl friends sitting expectantly in the stands, I waited anxiously near our end zone and watched the ball leave the tee on its long, arching flight upward. At the same time, eleven opponents charged down the field, ferociously intent on converging at one point: me. For a worrisome time I lost sight of the ball in the dark, then in the glare of the lights. It was an inconvenient moment to discover nearsightedness. When the ball suddenly came back into view, I misjudged its descent and it fell through my arms, then bounced erratically near the goal line. I scrambled frantically after it and finally scooped it up just before being mercilessly squashed by large, onrushing opponents. I spent the rest of the game on the bench, never started again, and was rarely sent in as a substitute. If my time had been valuable, I might have quit the sport in mid season, but I was propelled by the popular wisdom that "Winners never quit and quitters never win."

Football season became more agreeable when cross-country became a possibility, a development made possible by the fact that Ken Rio, the man who coached football in the fall, also coached track in the spring. We few runners who dabbled in football were excused from practice—our absence was no loss to the team—to form a little squad of six for cross-country meets. Running myself into exhaustion over the hills of a golf course was far preferable to pulling on all that heavy equipment and serving on the sacrificial "hamburger squad" against the much larger, harder hitting first team.

Basketball was even less rewarding than football. I played on the B team for a year or two, but I couldn't keep up with those players who in 1956 went on to win a state championship so I gave up the game for good. Watching from the stands, I found, was preferable to sitting shamefully on the bench or failing on the court, where I was never quite sure what to do or where to be. But football and basketball were just ways to mark time until track began in the spring when I could rededicate myself to the role of Runner with Olympian dreams. The track may have been the only place where I didn't feel like a fraud.

◆   ◆   ◆

The climate of the northern states is inhospitable to spring sports. The snow can linger until mid March, and ground frost sometimes prevented grooming the cinder track until weeks later, so in that long, awkward thawing time I conducted my own, early morning workouts near home. Rising just before dawn each school day, pulling on sweats, low-cut, rubber soled running shoes, stocking cap and gloves, I jogged down the hill and along the river to the golf course, arriving there when it was just light enough to see. In the early spring, the heavily frosted grass was steel-wool-stiff, and when the first signs of light made silhouettes of the cottonwoods along the river, you could see your breath. Starting slowly to warm up, I began jogging southward down the fairways and across the frozen greens, slowly picking up speed, feeling the muscles gradually loosen and relax, feeling the frosted grass crunch underfoot, gradually building speed and finally, as I neared the south end of the course, reaching a sprint. I jogged for a while, slow enough to recover my breath but fast enough to keep warm, then turned north for the return trip, repeating the drill and ending in a sprint up the hill toward the green at the end of the fourth fairway. For a warm-down, I jogged along the river toward home, then finished with one more sprint up the hill to the house just as the sun was starting to show.

It was almost impossible for me then to believe there were people who didn't like to run. At that point in my life, there was nothing better than taking off across the golf course alone on those cold spring mornings or running the back roads during summers at the lake, feeling light and free, propelled by my own power and my dream of fame in the Olympics. I never felt lighter and less encumbered than when I ran.

There were bad days, of course, when my arms and legs felt heavy and my whole body counteracted my will, but what I remember more are the days when my feet were barely touching the ground, as if I'd mysteriously overcome gravity and could keep going for miles. In most sports it's hard to see your progress from week to week, but from race to race I could measure my gains with wonderful precision and chart them in hundredths of seconds. I could train by myself if I liked, and my successes and failures were mine alone. How, I wondered, could anyone not like to run?

Besides, there was the chummy conviviality of meet days: meeting at the school early on Saturday morning; the long, drowsy ride on a Greyhound coach; sprawling on the infield grass with teammates while waiting for our events, occasionally getting up to cheer on a friend but otherwise reveling in adolescent banter about girls and wondering foolishly whether so-and-so had gotten laid the night before; the long ride home with thoughts of the sock hop that night at the "Y" and the last dance with the current love interest who couldn't wait to hear how I'd covered myself with glory that day on the field of competition.

Early in the season our high school team trained at the University field house where the chief attraction was rubbing elbows with runners from the University—strapping, hairy-chested, 20 year old men seemingly capable of astonishing feats of speed and endurance. But the air smelled dusty in there, and running on the cramped, un-banked, clay track with 12 laps to the mile was like running in circles, so it was a relief to finally move outdoors. But even then you can't count on fair weather in North Dakota; in one early-season meet, officials had to rake snow from the long jump pit before preliminaries could begin. With the short track season in the northern states and the inadequate indoor facilities, it isn't surprising that the country's track stars come from further south. North Dakota's high school records in track and field are almost as good as those in other states, but it's next to unheard-of for a North Dakota athlete to rise to the national level, let alone the Olympics.

But that fact didn't keep me from dreaming. I was idolizing the best runners in the world—sprinters like Bobby Morrow, half-milers like Mal Whitfield and Tom Courtney, and milers like Roger Banister and Herb Elliott—and I was dreaming of the Olympics.

Why shouldn't I? My teammates thought enough of me in my sophomore year to choose me co-captain along with Cliff Cushman, a recent transfer from Kansas, a bashful, quick-smiling, willowy runner who excelled at every running event and who a few years later would win a silver medal in the 400 meter hurdles at the 1960 Olympics in Rome. (I aped him by rejecting the standard spikes issued by the school in favor of the white, kangaroo skin shoes imported from Australia.) Besides, running the 440 again, I placed in five meets that season—including two firsts, one of them a meet record—and steadily pared fractions of seconds from my previous times. We won the state championship, thanks in part to my second place finish and Cliff's firsts in the high and low hurdles and mile.

As a junior, running the 440 and occasionally a medley relay, I finished first or second in every meet but one, and with Cliff winning four events at the state meet (high and low hurdles, long jump and mile)—three of them with state records—we were state champions again. It should have been an omen to me that even though I'd cut a full two and a half seconds off my time in the state meet of the previous year, I was still stuck in second place. But by ignoring it, and with hope and perseverance—the latter defined by Ambrose Bierce as "a lowly virtue whereby mediocrity achieves an inglorious success"—I was able to sustain my Olympian dreams and my expectations of a college track scholarship the following year.

Early in the spring of my senior year, in one of the first outdoor practices of the season, a muscle injury forced me to abandon the event I'd spent three years learning. In spite of treatments from a physical therapist at Pop's clinic, I couldn't sprint; I had to drop the 440 and find a race that didn't call for speed. We didn't need any help in the mile—with Cliff, we had one of the top high school milers in the country—so all that was left was the 880. The 880, I soon found, was a more attractive distance for me than the 440, a race that allowed more time for strategy and maneuvering, more time to enjoy the thrill of running, maybe even time to overcome a mistake in tactics. I liked this new race and wished I'd found it earlier, and I continued to learn how to run it and to pare away seconds from meet to meet. Even though I finished second each time behind Jack Lutes, a tall, lumbering, long-legged runner from Fargo, the top half-miler in the state, I was steadily lowering my time and shrinking the gap between us. And even though Jack beat me again in the eastern division meet, the prelude to the state meet, I'd closed the gap enough to know that in the state meet I'd pass him with 60 yards to go and take the first place I wanted so badly.

In practices leading up to the final meet, I worked almost exclusively on speed, sprinting again and again around that first curve and practicing a form of constructive self-delusion well known to runners: conditioning myself to a pace that would seem annoyingly slow when the actual race began.

Some runners, those with bravado and a hell-bent style, move right to the front and dare others to challenge them; others prefer to hang back watchfully. A hanger-back, I planned to fall into second place at the start of the back stretch, close enough to my lumbering, long-legged friend from Fargo that I could reach out and touch him, running just off his right shoulder to make it tougher for others to pass.

On the day of the race—in my memory, it was the only race that day—the track-side rumor was that another 880 runner, Pat Keller, a sophomore from the Western part of the state, an unknown entity to me, a guy who was said to get his training by running from police, would begin his kick *not* as he was coming out of the final curve toward the tape when I would start mine, but much earlier, with almost 300 yards to go. The mark of an over-eager, under-experienced runner, I thought. Let him.

In my four years of high school track and all the years before that, I ran more than 60 races. All are a blur but the last, a race I re-ran many times to see if it might come out different. Many details of that race are still clear, and the outcome is always the same.

Each race began the same way, with a mass of congealed anxiety in the pit of the stomach. The mass grew throughout the day of the race, and as I finally stepped into my assigned lane and waited impatiently for the starter's commands, as I thought about the exhaustion I'd feel at the end—the pain in the chest, the rubbery lifelessness in the arms and legs—I wondered why I put myself through this again and again. But then the gun went off and that burdensome lump exploded; the tension that had been building throughout the day was suddenly released, somehow turned into energy, and my body was mysteriously, miraculously, and dramatically charged. In an instant the race was on, dread and anxiety were transformed into exhilaration, and I no longer questioned why I was there, no longer doubted that I loved to run.

The race began fast, as I knew it would, and after the first 200 hundred yards I fell comfortably into second place behind Jack where I wanted to be, running light and relaxed, excited but still calmly at ease, the front-runner in reach, the others out of my mind, and for much of the two-lap race, oblivious to the noise from the stands, I relished the incomparable sense of being in charge. At the start of the last lap we couldn't hear the timer—only the gun and the crowd—but I'd developed a sense of pace and by this time hardly need the clock; I knew the pace was excitingly fast.

As we were approaching the backstretch of the final lap with 300 yards to go, I was still comfortably and confidently in second place when Keller made his move and sped past us both to take over the race. Tempted for a moment to go with him, I let him go, reminding myself that he'd fade in the end, that he wasn't the one to beat.

Coming out of the last curve, still feeling strong, still where I'd wanted to be, I made my move to the outside and began my sprint, passing Jack and aiming now at the young runner Keller in first. At this moment, my mental re-running of the event suddenly goes to slow motion, the last 50 yards taking longer to replay than everything up to that point. My vision had started to blur and it was hard to judge distance, but now, with nobody between us, the lead runner seemed surprisingly far away—in the 50 yards I had left, maybe too far to reach. In that last 50-yard sprint, when my legs got leaden and my energy was dwindling toward zero, when my mind was telling my body to resist all those terrible instincts to tighten up, I told myself in increasingly frantic terms that the gap was narrowing, that his legs were rubbery, that he was wobbling in his lane, that he was slowly fading back towards me, a victim of his own inexperience and foolish bravado, that he would wither before me and that I, the savvy old runner with the experience of all those state meets behind me, would pass him in the end and be first in the state.

It didn't happen. Keller wasn't fading at all. He finished first, in under two minutes—almost two, long, disheartening seconds ahead of me. Not only had I failed to reach the first place goal I'd set three years earlier, I'd been beaten by a runner two years younger than I. Scrambling for consolation, I found a little in having run a personal best, in beating a runner I'd never beaten before, and in breaking the school record my friend Cliff had set the previous year. But it didn't help much. If I'd had any sense of perspective at all, I'd have taken satisfaction in having qualified for the state meet four years straight and having finished second in three of them; but the only reality I could see was the failure to finish first. Second-best was counterfeit currency.

A few weeks after the season was over I went back to the University track once more. With one friend as a timer and another to pace me in the second lap, I wanted to beat the sophomore's first place time at the state meet, figuring it might help repair my tattered ego, or at least break two minutes. I didn't do either. I cut six tenths of a second off my earlier, school-record time, but it was unofficial, a time trial, and counted for nothing.

No offers of track scholarships came that spring either. It was another in childhood's series of lurches and leaps: the realization that by dreaming of glory in the world of track I'd once again been spinning childish fantasies. Those fantasies hadn't been useless, of course; they'd helped impel me through several years of training, helped me muster the self-discipline it takes to go out and run, especially on days when I'd rather not. They were at the root of my earlier successes in the sport and of the identity I'd enjoyed through that otherwise shaky, uncertain period of adolescence. But like so many childish dreams, it promised something beyond my reach, and when it was demolished it left an unsettling void.

If I'd prepared myself for the possibility of losing, or if I'd been able to rank the loss with my earlier childhood disappointments—my failure to get rich trapping mink and selling magazines, my disillusion over the Charles Atlas body building scheme, the unfulfilled dream of joining a professional water-ski troupe—I could have made it a lot easier for myself and been less inclined than I was to see this as the end of the world.

◆   ◆   ◆

Sitting through our commencement ceremony in the Central High School auditorium on a late-May morning of 1957, one of 187 graduates sweltering in our cumbersome caps and gowns, I watched as *other* class members gave the speeches, received the academic prizes, sang the solos, and directed the chorus in "You'll Never Walk Alone." ("Every time a friend succeeds, I die a little," as Gore Vidal said.) That morning I had the discomforting sense that for much of my adolescence I'd been deluding myself, that I'd been overestimating my talent or underestimating the effort it takes to develop it, that in funneling all my resources into that single dream of the Olympics, I'd been building a castle without enough bricks. As Oscar Levant said, it's not who you are, it's what you don't become that hurts.

In my own narrow, somewhat distorted view of myself, the identity I'd been carefully cultivating for years had suddenly crumpled on the track at Valley City. At the time, of course, it seemed cataclysmic. If after all those years I wasn't to be an Olympic runner, wasn't even the best in my event in North Dakota, couldn't even beat a balding, middle-aged guy in a sprint, then who was I? I'd already accepted that I was mediocre in other sports, that I didn't have the talent or the aptitude for leadership, that I had no inclination to scholarship. Now once again I felt I'd been playing a role for which I'd been miscast, but this time the pain of discovery was far more acute because I'd chosen that role myself and put all my stock in it, and because now I had no idea who I was. In the long, arduous, ragged, haphazard enterprise of creating a self, I would have to start over.

◆   ◆   ◆

Our commencement speaker that spring—like his counterparts all over the country—emphasized the smorgasbord of opportunities spread out before us in those unusually prosperous times. "The doors are open to you," he said. "The world is at your feet." In 1957 they could say that with conviction. There weren't many impediments to us as we looked into our futures. For those of us headed to college, admission was easy and tuition was low—ninety dollars a semester at our state universities; for others, employment was high and jobs were abundant, and there was always military service, which wasn't a bad deal in that time of peace.

I was headed for the University of North Dakota, marching lockstep with most of my friends, not giving much thought about *why* or *to what end* but having blind faith that in some miraculous way those questions would somehow answer themselves. The important thing was that all that high school kid stuff was behind me—the proms, the clubs, student government, all that fol de rol; I was naively moving on to what I thought was the all-serious, grown-up world of higher education.

In those rosy times, it would have been hard to be anything but optimistic, hard not to have faith that in spite of the dawn of the nuclear age, the ubiquitous threat of communism, and the oncoming wave of racial turmoil, on the whole, American life would just get better and better, or at least stay as good as it was. So I had that going for me, and the certainty that whatever my talents, society would reward hard work with material success. Our homogenous, morally and religiously conservative climate had fortified me with the ability to distinguish right from wrong and to know that the former would invariably prevail, and somehow it had bred into me the sense that I was responsible for myself, for whoever I was and whoever I might become.

But there is another side to this legacy. We Upper Midwesterners have absorbed from our peculiar environment certain precepts, certain strictures that have all the ominous power and authority of commandments. *Thou shalt not put thy emotions on display*, says one of them. *Thou shalt bury thy anger and disappointments, thy joys and affections. Whatsoever thy pains and frustrations, thou shalt inflict them on others not.*

Thou shalt not pry into thy neighbor's life, says another. *Nor shalt thou ask about his politics or his religion, especially at the dinner table, where strong feelings are inappropriate and interfere with digestion. Privacy is a virtue that cannot be carried to excess.*

Thou shalt not be ostentatious. If thou hast money, more power to thee, but thou shalt not flaunt it, nor shall thou even appear to enjoy its advantages.

And finally, *Thou shalt not complain. Thou shalt accept the winter cold and snow and snirt and the spring floods and the summer heat and the grasshoppers because complaining is fruitless and unseemly, and besides, the tribulations of others may greatly exceed thine own.*

These commandments weren't posted on church doors or schoolroom walls, of course; they weren't recited from pulpits or lecterns or the heads of dinner tables; they weren't even written down. But they were heavy in the air around us; we absorbed them as unconsciously as we do our native language, and they trailed us into adulthood where they became the ground rules for all our social intercourse, including friendships and even marriage. They formed a major part of who we are, as integral to our personalities as genes to our physical selves, and they trail us all our lives.

Somehow by the end of our high school years Mom and Pop had ensured that my brothers and I, although still dependent financially, could otherwise stand on our own without parental supports or buttresses. Rather than steer us by direct or remote control through the thorny underbrush of childhood and adolescence, rather than protect us from our inclinations to folly, they'd left us alone to bumble into our own stupidities, then find our own way out, ensuring that in spite of our material comfort, growing up would be an eventful journey. I don't know if it had been a conscious child-rearing strategy or an accident of benign neglect, but they hadn't been omnipresent figures in our growing up, as I can see by sorting through these memories. They'd left us pretty much to ourselves. As Mom put it years later, "Your father and I always figured that you boys had your lives and we had ours."

("Is it true," as Reeve Lindbergh asks about her famous family, "that all parents are too busy to pay full attention to their children? Or is the truth instead that no child can ever be satisfied, because no child can have every ounce of a parent's attention? Do we all imagine ourselves, whether we are teenagers, middle-aged, or octogenarians, as insufficiently appreciated as children?")

In my growing up, I see more clearly now, my parents were less and less the center of my life, and by sorting through these memories, I can see that Paul and Don are conspicuously absent too, a fact that surprised me only at first. Paul was actually in the thick of the neighborhood activities of our elementary school years—the sandlot football, baseball and hockey games, the underground caves by the river, the crab apple crimes and all the rest of it; but he was two years ahead of me in school, and by junior high we began developing our own interests and our own groups of friends.

Don, five and a half years younger than I, too young to be part of our neighborhood games, was in my childhood little more than a figure of curiosity and occasional amusement. It wasn't until I was 22, when he was a high school sophomore and got kicked off the hockey team for drinking, when he withdrew his money from the bank and surreptitiously boarded a Greyhound bus for Denver while Mom and Pop were in Minneapolis celebrating their twenty-fifth anniversary, that I really began to notice him.

Now here's an interesting kid, I thought, a kid with daring and imagination. But I could also see that he was a kid with a problem: He'd taken up drinking, he'd lost a tooth in a fight at the gravel pits, and even at 16 he was developing a morose view of the world, a propensity to ask, "Is this all there is to life?" But in our family we never talked about Don's running away or about the unhappiness that lay behind it. I'm sure Mom and Pop worried plenty about Don; they even arranged for him to see a psychiatrist—a drastic measure in those days. But that was it. We never talked about it as a family. It was our way to stash these kinds of things in a closet, and the result was that we never learned how to talk with each other about what mattered most. We still haven't. As a family, we remain cordial but politely distant, dodging subjects that might give us discomfort, reluctant to probe, pleasantly unaware of each other's disappointments and troubles.

Pop was even more distant than anyone else. As a physician, he was an effective provider of material comforts—we had the summer cabin at the lake and family trips, and we always had nice cars and nice clothes, and there was money for summer camp and for braces on crooked teeth—but it would have been quite a stretch to call him a comforter or a nurturer. He certainly taught me how to hold a gun, how to "lead" a duck with both eyes open, how to squeeze the trigger gently rather than pull. He taught me how to insert a fishhook through the minnow's mouth, then thread it out the gill and through the meaty part of the back; how to attach a 5/8 sinker, how to let out line until I hit bottom, then reel in a few turns. He taught me to obey the rules and not take more game than I'd eat. But as far as I could see he never seemed to take much pleasure in any of this, either in his teaching or in our learning. Fishing at the lake, time we might have spent trying to understand each other, we'd spend an hour or two together alone in the boat without much more than a "Please pass the minnows."

The driving lessons were especially awkward. The thrilling prospect of a driver's license and the mobility it provides was offset by the tension I felt in the car with him. In our large, navy blue Buick Roadmaster with automatic transmission, he took me to a gravel road south of town by a muddy slough we called Greenwood Lake, then shut off the engine and instructed me to change places with him. Sitting in the driver's seat with the steering wheel in my uncertain hands, I was suddenly amazed at how much car stuck out both in front of me and behind.

"Turn the key to start the engine. Now, put your foot on the brake, put the gear shift into 'Drive,' and slowly take your foot off the brake," he said, at the same time putting his right leg against the floorboards, his left arm over the seat back, and his right arm against the dashboard, as if to prepare for a certain collision.

Even without my foot on the gas, the car moved faster than I'd expected.

"Watch the right edge of the road there. Watch the edge, watch the edge, you're too close to the ditch."

I turned to the left but overcompensated.

"You turned too far. You turned too far. Back to the right. Back to the right."

When I was creeping along in a fairly straight line, "Now put on the break."

I did, and we jerked to an uncomfortable stop, Pop lurching forward and almost hitting his head on the dash.

"Not so hard. Not so hard. You're stopping too fast. Squeeze the break slowly. You don't have to jam it."

Impatient, irritable, tense, he clearly didn't cherish either the role of driving instructor or the prospect of our time together, and instead of putting me at ease behind the wheel and building my confidence as a driver, his instruction did the opposite. As he had in our religious training, he gave me the feeling he was carrying out an unwelcome chore.

At the end of that first lesson, he might have said, "You're doing fine; it just takes some practice." Or, "Don't worry about the mistakes; we all make them at first." But in my memory, he says nothing. (As Anne Sexton says, "It doesn't matter who my father was; it matters who I remember he was.")

Our contacts were always perfunctory. As I look over my report cards from 12 years of school, I note that it was always Pop's role to sign them, yet I don't remember his ever wanting to talk about my school work, ever wondering what I thought, ever asking questions that might lead to friendly, casual discussion. If one of his sons put forth an idea at dinner, he was apt to dismiss it rather than probe our minds and encourage some give and take. He was inclined to pronouncements, and his pronouncements usually ended the matter.

In my second year at the University, when I was lionizing Hemmingway and had been captivated by his novels, I convinced Pop—who never picked up fiction—to read *The Sun Also Rises*. We were at the lake when he finished the book. He was lying on the same couch from which he'd challenged me to the race. He threw the book down in disgust. "It's nothing but a story about a guy whose balls are shot off in the war," he said. I couldn't see any point in trying to discuss it with him, but I *could* see that the gap between us—the gap between the practical, hardheaded physician and the son who was on the verge of becoming a student and teacher of literature—was growing and growing.

I think he watched me run a few times—I know he and Mom came to my last state meet—but I don't remember his ever asking me about running, ever complimenting me on a first place finish or consoling me in a loss. He never seemed to take vicarious pleasure in my accomplishments and never was curious about my dreams. He seemed to be observing my brothers and me from a distance, as if we were somebody else's children. That's why it was particularly painful a few years later to watch him engage in long conversations with classmates of mine who were considering careers in medicine, friends who are doctors now and who years later still cherish the time and advice he gave them.

During that prolonged phase of self-centeredness called childhood and adolescence, and for many years after that, I puzzled over his seeming disinterest in trying to understand me. What's going on here? Wasn't that part of his job as a father? It was decades later when I finally woke to the fact I hadn't done any better, that I'd made no effort to understand him either, that we were equally at fault, and that just as he had patiently counseled those friends of mine who wanted to go into medicine, years later as a teacher I also found it easier sometimes to be father to someone else's children.

So eventually I came to understand that even in his fifties he was still constrained by his own Victorian childhood and by those same strictures of our Upper Midwestern, Scandinavian-Lutheran conservatism, that maybe he was raising his sons as his father had raised him. Just as I felt unsuited for some of the roles I'd tried, maybe as a father he too had been playing a role for which he felt miscast, a role that demands a capacity for warmth and intimacy that his own childhood had never let him achieve. It all made sense when I finally realized what maybe I should have understood much earlier: that he had grown up in the same place I did, that he had been subjected to those same unwritten commandments, that he too was constrained by the climate of his childhood world. That he was a Dakota boy too.

As I said before, growing up is a prolonged struggle to overcome one thing or another, and sometimes it's hard not to believe that one of the things we must all overcome is our fathers. But now, almost 15 years after that long-ago scene in the nursing home when he tried so hard to speak, just as I'm entering old age myself, I think I'm finally beginning to understand him, to stretch a too-late hand across the canyon of time, to make allowances for the shortcomings a father isn't supposed to have. And I've come to admit that it's not just our fathers we have to overcome; it's ourselves.

But another burden—one that would tail me just as long—came with my small town isolation on the Northern Plains. I couldn't have known it at the time but life's currents would inevitably float me further a field where, like country folks just arrived in the city, I'd discover a nagging, inescapable sense of cultural inferiority. My response would be a posture of defensiveness, an impulse to retreat to what I knew, to the circumscribed, mono-cultural world that felt familiar and safe. To break out of that world takes either an act of will or a simmering discontent; eventually I would have both, but at that point I had neither.

Even though I'd established a healthy degree of independence from parents, I wasn't yet independent from friends; like a fish in a school, I stayed in formation, swerving this way or that with the rest, too cautious to make my own judgments, to dare to zig left when they were zagging right. Even though as a high school junior and a prudish, strait-laced co-captain of the track team I turned in a teammate who'd been drinking and who was promptly kicked off the team, I'm not sure I'd have done the same if he'd been one of my friends.

Probably like most high school graduates, I was unburdened by a serious sense of purpose and knew little of how little I knew. But in retrospect, especially after this excursion into the cave of memory, I know I had the luxury of an untroubled childhood filled with opportunities I'm happy to have had, a childhood that left me with memories I hoard—the riverside years of sliding and playing hockey and digging subterranean huts and hunting and trapping; the summers at Bemidji; the travel, the hunting trips with family and the camping trips with classmates; the camaraderie of sports, the pleasures of cruising through those early years with friends who are still friends today. Maybe old age will surpass it, but so far I'd say that for me, childhood may be the greatest adventure of all, and that these memories of it, both good and bad, constitute my greatest inheritance.

Even though I was going on to the University that fall, I hadn't given much thought to *why*. To tell the truth, beyond the state track meet I hadn't given much thought to anything at all. Was I much different from anyone else? Has there ever been a high school graduate who didn't wish he'd studied more and given more thought to his future? I stare back longingly over the chasm of years at the might-have-beens, lamenting the false paths I chose, the opportunities I let slip by, suspecting that I probably gained by my errors but at the same time wondering where I might be without them, and recognizing that to some degree, as Calvin Trillin says, everyone is who he was in high school.

Luckily, the personae we wear in that long, ragged process of growing up, whether we donned them ourselves or had them draped over us, are just temporary guises. We try on each one in turn, look at ourselves in the mirror to see if it fits, wear it around for a while, then toss it aside or—Houdini-like—escape it before moving on to the next. We'll try on several more before we're through, and we're probably adults by the time we find a good fit, one that we can wear in comfort for the rest of our lives. And it might be many years more before we finally turn around and look back, before we creep cautiously into the cave of memory and sift through those remains of childhood to examine those clues to who we were, who we are, and to wonder *Why*. But even then it's not too late.

About the Author

Robert Woutat, a North Dakota native, is an award-winning columnist with *The Sun*, the daily newspaper in Bremerton, Washington. He has been a teacher, a wilderness guide, a freelance writer and humorist, and, under the name of Dr. Grammarian, a contributor to KPLU radio, the NPR affiliate in Seattle/Tacoma.

0-595-28447-7